"Psychoanalysis is about courage – courage to face distressin[g in a] class of discussing perhaps the most painful reality of all – t[he] decline and ultimate ephemerality. This is a rare and immens[e help] and students facing an ageing population who turn to us in increasing numbers demanding and deserving psychological support. The book is rich with practical but remarkably gentle instruction on how this can be provided to the greatest benefit of both those asking for support and those who wish to offer it. This book, in addition to being scholarly and massively helpful, is above all, extraordinarily compassionate and equally empowering for therapists and clients. A major achievement of clinical skill from one of the major expert innovators in the field."

Professor Peter Fonagy, *OBE FMedSci FBA FacSS, Head of the Division of Psychology and Language Sciences, University College London; Chief Executive, Anna Freud National Centre for Children & Families*

"This brave and moving book draws on the author's long clinical engagement with both individuals and couples in their later years, facing the many losses of old age and the reality of death's approach. Andrew Balfour's scholarly grasp of psychoanalytic practice and its many theoretical roots is combined with a deep love of literature, especially poetry, and with solid knowledge of the contemporary conditions of old people's lives and close and original study of the impact of dementia. It is a most impressive achievement, confronting readers with the painfulness of ageing but also with the human capacity to live in touch with our mortality if we can feel accompanied both within and without. It should be read very widely as our whole society needs to think afresh about how to create better lives and dignified deaths for old people."

Margaret Rustin, *Honorary Consultant Child and Adolescent Psychotherapist, Tavistock and Portman NHS Trust, Child Analyst, British Psychoanalytic Society*

"This beautiful book demonstrates the possibility of psychic development in spite of the extreme constraints of limited time. It exposes painful dilemmas for the therapist, yet the moving clinical work frequently involves repairing the apparently irreparable."

Anne Alvarez *Consultant Child and Adolescent Psychotherapist*

"*Life and Death* delivers gold mined from Andrew Balfour's career-long study of older individuals and couples. Many clinicians shy away from this arena, but Balfour offers a dazzling array of clinical and theoretical pathways to understanding its travails alongside the possibilities for providing care for the aged. He brings his years of experience and his compassion to this examination of difficulties inherent in intimacy and sexuality, multiple physical and mental losses, family struggle, and the vicissitudes of dementia. This book unearths gems from the previously unexplored continent of ageing. For us clinicians who encounter ever more old individuals and couples, this book will serve as an inspiring guide."

David E. Scharff, *MD; Director Emeritus, International Psychotherapy Institute; Recipient, The Mary Sigourney Award for the Advancement of Psychoanalysis; co-editor, Psychoanalytic Couple Therapy*

"If, as Kafka said, the meaning of life is that it stops, this accessible book addresses unspoken fears and fantasies about loss of capacity, and the emotional challenges of later life. Drawing on vivid literary examples and a wealth of clinical experience, Andrew Balfour fosters both self-reflection and truthful communication in intimate relationships (even when one partner has dementia).."

Professor Joan Raphael-Leff, *PhD [Retired], Fellow, British Psychoanalytical Society Leader, Academic Faculty for Psychoanalytic Research, Anna Freud Centre London; Honorary Senior Research Fellow, UCL*

Life and Death

Life and Death considers ageing and mortality from a psychoanalytic perspective and from the point of view of the individual, the couple, and the family.

Andrew Balfour's approach focuses on understanding the challenges of late life and what might help us to continue to live our lives, and inhabit our relationships, as creatively as possible. The book grounds a psychoanalytic approach to understanding later life as a key point of developmental challenge for us all, through closely written accounts of the experiences of older people, as well as wider social-contextual issues. It locates itself at the interface of internal and external realities, exploring the lived experience of some of the most difficult things we can face in old age, such as dementia and other age-related illnesses and losses.

Life and Death will be of interest to psychoanalysts, psychotherapists, counsellors, and psychologists in practice and in training. It will also appeal to the general reader interested in ageing and the challenges of late life.

Andrew Balfour trained as a clinical psychologist at University College London and then as an adult psychotherapist at the Tavistock & Portman NHS Trust. He subsequently trained as a couple psychotherapist at Tavistock Relationships, where for more than 10 years he was clinical director before becoming chief executive in 2016.

The Library of Couple and Family Psychoanalysis

Series Editors: Christopher Clulow, Brett Kahr, Elizabeth Palacios and David Scharff

The library offers the best of psychoanalytically informed writing on adult partnerships and couple psychotherapy. A full list of the titles in the series can be found at https://www.routledge.com/The-Library-of-Couple-and-Family-Psychoanalysis/book-series/KARNLCFP.

Recent titles in the series:

Couple Stories: Application of Psychoanalytic Ideas in Thinking About Couple Interaction
Edited by Aleksandra Novakovic and Marguerite Reid.

Clinical Dialogues on Psychoanalysis with Families and Couples
Edited by David E. Scharff and Monica Vorchheimer

Family and Couple Psychoanalysis: A Global Perspective
Edited by David E. Scharff and Elizabeth Palacios

What Makes Us Stay Together? Attachment and the Outcomes of Couple Relationships
Rosetta Castellano, Patrizia Velotti and Giulio Cesare Zavattini

Psychoanalytic Couple Therapy: Foundations of Theory and Practice
Edited by David E. Scharff and Jill Savage Scharff

How Couple Relationships Shape our World: Clinical Practice, Research, and Policy Perspectives
Edited by Andrew Balfour, Mary Morgan and Christopher Vincent

Sex, Attachment and Couple Psychotherapy: Psychoanalytic Perspectives
Edited by Christopher Clulow

Life and Death: Our Relationship with Ageing, Dementia, and Other Fates of Time
Andrew Balfour

Life and Death

Our Relationship with Ageing, Dementia, and Other Fates of Time

Andrew Balfour

LONDON AND NEW YORK

Designed cover image: Andrew Hasson / Alamy Stock Photo

First published 2025
by Routledge
4 Park Square, Milton Park, Abingdon, Oxon OX14 4RN

and by Routledge
605 Third Avenue, New York, NY 10158

Routledge is an imprint of the Taylor & Francis Group, an informa business

© 2025 Andrew Balfour

The right of Andrew Balfour to be identified as author of this work has been asserted in accordance with sections 77 and 78 of the Copyright, Designs and Patents Act 1988.

All rights reserved. No part of this book may be reprinted or reproduced or utilised in any form or by any electronic, mechanical, or other means, now known or hereafter invented, including photocopying and recording, or in any information storage or retrieval system, without permission in writing from the publishers.

Trademark notice: Product or corporate names may be trademarks or registered trademarks, and are used only for identification and explanation without intent to infringe.

British Library Cataloguing in Publication Data
A catalogue record for this book is available from the British Library

ISBN: 9781032636481 (hbk)
ISBN: 9781032636467 (pbk)
ISBN: 9781032636498 (ebk)

DOI: 10.4324/9781032636498

Typeset in Times New Roman
by Taylor & Francis Books

To my parents Fred and Joan Balfour, and my children – Emily, Sebastian, and Anna Rose. My brother and sister, Tim, and Melissa. And to my wife, Deborah, whose thoughts are so much a part of this book.

Contents

	Acknowledgements	xi
	Introduction	xiii
1	Ageing in Body and Mind: The Challenges of Living a Long Life	1
2	Intimacy and Sexuality in Later Life	20
3	Another Country?: Migration, Displacement, and Internal Dislocation in Old Age	37
4	Thinking about the Experience of Dementia: The Importance of the Unconscious Mind	56
5	The Fragile Thread of Connection: Living as a Couple with Dementia	75
6	Working Psychotherapeutically with Couples Who Are Living with Dementia	91
7	At Home in a Home?: Institutional Care and the 'Unheimlich'	108
8	Dying and Assisted Death	119
	Index	135

We must speak of failure, abomination, and death, not to drive our readers to despair, but on the contrary, to try to save them from despair.
– Simone de Beauvoir, 'What Can Literature Do?', 1965

Acknowledgements

Most of the books in the world contain words spoken to us from beyond the grave. Looking at my bookshelf the other day, I was struck by how many of the authors of the books I have treasured are now dead. Many more of them than when their books were first put on the shelves. And yet, how their words still live. Our wish not to be forgotten, by leaving behind some part of ourselves – in the minds of family and friends, or an imagined readership, is perhaps a wishful hope to manage the reality of our time-limited lives. There is, I think, such a motivation for me in writing this book, which expresses my efforts to learn from the people I have worked with – who have taught me so much about life, in facing illness and death. I have often noticed the striking emotional capacities of the colleagues I have met working in the field of late life. I must thank Rachel Davenhill, whose writing I first encountered when I was a student and with whom I then had the good fortune to work at the Tavistock Clinic, where together we established the 'Psychodynamic Approaches to Old Age' course. We had many wonderful participants, and we were supported by colleagues such as Margaret Rustin, Margot Waddell, Anne Amos (whose clinical supervision was so helpful in developing this work), and many others. I must also thank Peter and Jessica Hobson, who started supervising my long-running PhD, which developed the Living Together with Dementia intervention – it was their ideas that were central to this. I'd like to thank Peter Fonagy, who supervised this PhD project for many years, for his tremendous generosity and support – which goes back a long way to my training in clinical psychology at UCL where the work described in these pages began. At Tavistock Relationships, I was supported to develop the Living Together with Dementia project by Susanna Abse and Honor Rhodes. Liz Salter was my great companion in those early pioneering days, and Beth Winter, Ann Kelly, and Rebeca Robertson have also been deeply committed colleagues. My wife, Deborah Farrell, has been part of this journey since the beginning. From staying up late at night helping with conference presentations, to critical readings of, and creative contributions to, the papers I have written over the years. Her deep psychoanalytic understanding has been key, and I am forever grateful for her loving devotion of her talents in helping me to develop the ideas which you will read about in this book. The many patients I have had the privilege of working with are a central presence in this text and I hope that my gratitude to them is clear to the reader throughout. My thanks to Holly Ingram and Katie Torres at Tavistock Relationships, and the editors at Routledge – Susannah Frearson, Saloni Singhania, and Hamish Ironside – who helped, invaluably, in getting this book produced. And to my friends of a lifetime – especially Mick, Sarah, Rupert, and Adam.

An earlier version of Chapter 1 was originally published as 'Growing Old Together in Mind and Body', chapter 14 in S. Nathans and M. Schaefer (eds), *Couples on the Couch: Psychoanalytic Couple Therapy and the Tavistock Model*, pp. 221–244, Routledge, 2017. Reproduced by permission of Taylor & Francis Group.

Chapter 2 was originally published as 'Intimacy and Sexuality in Old Age', chapter 12 in C. Clulow (ed.), *Sex, Attachment and Couple Psychotherapy*, pp. 217–237, Routledge, 2009. Reproduced by permission of Taylor & Francis Group.

An earlier version of Chapter 3 was originally published as 'Another Country? Migration, Displacement, and Internal Dislocation in Old Age', chapter 6 in A. Varchevker and E. McGinley (eds), *Enduring Migration Through the Lifespan*, pp. 106–133, Routledge, 2013. Reproduced by permission of Taylor & Francis Group.

An earlier version of Chapter 4 originally appeared as 'Thinking about the Experience of Dementia: The Importance of the Unconscious Mind', *Journal of Social Work Practice*, 20(3) (2006), 329–346 (doi:10.1080/02650530600931914). Reproduced by permission of Taylor & Francis Group.

Chapter 5 was originally published as 'The Fragile Thread of Connection: Living as a Couple with Dementia', chapter 10 in S. Evans, J. Garner, and R. Darnley-Smith (eds), *Psychodynamic Approaches to Old Age*, pp. 118–133, Routledge, 2020. Reproduced by permission of Taylor & Francis Group.

Thanks to Fitzcarraldo Editions and Pushkin Press for permission to quote from Simone de Beauvoir and Stefan Zweig, respectively

Introduction

> ... now I am Six, I'm as clever as clever,
> So I think I'll be six now for ever and ever.
> – A. A. Milne, *Now We Are Six*

Do you remember school, when, if you were six and your friend was five and a half, it really mattered? When having had another birthday meant that you were much bigger than them. Then, in younger adulthood, your friends' birthdays being months, maybe even a few years, apart from yours made little difference. But how all this changes as you age. Suddenly, it matters again. Friends from school sound like they did all those years ago – though now, the tables are turned. No longer am I flaunting my turning another year older a few months ahead of them. Now, they claim, they are 'much younger' than me – as they are still to reach my Significant Milestone. I am now in my sixties. In my mind's eye, I hear you, the reader, gasp. 'What, *you*, in your sixties? How can one so young, with so much promise, really have reached that age?' Simone de Beauvoir (1972, p. 316) wrote: 'Within me it is the Other – that is the person I am for the outsider – who is old ...'. In old age, in herself, she felt as she had always done. The unwelcome reality of ageing was refracted back to her in the eyes of the Other. Each year, the new students I teach look younger. Ageing can be felt to be happening 'in reverse' – we do not age, others get younger. As the world recedes from us, into an ever more youthful state, we may feel we stay still, marooned in time. Our often-troubled relationship with ageing is the subject of this book.

It is something most of us would rather not think about. Who wants to notice our journey towards death, which is signalled to us in the changes brought by the passage of time? If you are about to put this book back on the shelf with a shudder – stop! Wait a moment. If you read on, you might find something of the inspiration I have encountered over the years, from people I have known – friends, patients and colleagues – meeting, close-up, with their capacity to engage deeply with their experience in facing the most profound human challenges: the loss of physical and mental functioning and impending mortality – the ultimate vulnerabilities of our human condition.

At times, I have thought of their accounts as 'dispatches from the front', from the very edge of human experiencing. If we can bear to travel with them, we might be helped to understand more of what it is to be ourselves: sentient beings who are conscious of our limited lives and of the most profound losses which may overtake us – above all, perhaps, the prospect of losing memory – the very essence of all that we are and have been. This is the human situation within which we try to find ways of sustaining ourselves and our relationships with others.

As we age, every one of us is faced with loss. And, as we lose our physical capacities and mental agility, ordinary things, the trip to visit a friend, the journey to the local shops, can become fraught with challenges. Above all, the threat of what we might call the 'catastrophes' of old age, such as stroke or dementia, looms larger as we get older – the odds shifting against us. Whether or not they become our lived reality, these fates wait in the wings as possibilities for us and those we love, a troubling presence that is a backdrop to our lives. Our ability to maintain our reflective capacities in the face of this may wax and wane. I think the best we can hope for is that some of the time, perhaps, we may have sufficient internal support to find a tolerance for the anxieties of ageing and the ultimate loss of death and the end of our time. This book is about ageing and mortality from the point of view of our relationships. Its focus is on understanding the challenges of late life and what might help us to continue to live our lives, and inhabit our relationships, as creatively as possible. My approach is to ground a psychoanalytic understanding of later life as a key point of developmental challenge for us all, in closely written accounts of the experiences of older individuals and couples, as well as wider social-contextual issues. This book locates itself at the interface of internal and external realities – exploring the experience of some of the most difficult things we can face in old age, such as dementia and other illnesses and losses. Overall, it takes the view that finding the capacity to engage emotionally with these 'facts of life' may be fundamental to holding onto an authentic contact with our own experience and creativity, and retaining the ability to be ourselves, to the end of our lives.

On Our Hatred of Old Age

The way we responded as a society to the Covid-19 pandemic is a powerful illustration of our hatred of old age, and exploring this for a few pages now is a way for us to begin thinking about the psychological difficulties ageing presents. I began writing and editing this book at the start of the pandemic, at a time when people around the world were isolating and dying, and older people were among the most vulnerable. We are challenged by the prospect of ageing and mortality and, as a society, we adopt various defensive measures. This was writ large by the events of the pandemic. Although I will be discussing the response to the pandemic in the UK, the issues I shall describe are, I believe, relevant internationally. To this end, I will draw on newspaper articles that I collected over the course of the pandemic, which I think help to bring back to life that extraordinary time, which is now receding from us, into history.

Do you remember how it was at the beginning? Every day the radio brought news of more deaths – often that another well-known celebrity, who we hadn't heard about for a while, had died. 'Oh yes, they must be old now', I would find myself thinking, as the broadcast went on. And sure enough, the radio announcer always confirmed their age, adding 'after developing symptoms of Covid-19'. All the early announcements of deaths from Covid mentioned the age of the person concerned, and that they 'had underlying health conditions'. 'Phew', one was presumably supposed to feel – 'that's not us – perhaps they were going to die soon anyway' – as I overheard someone in the street saying at the time, on one of my lockdown walks. The dead were in the category of 'other' – older people, who were in any case at a 'die-able' age. Although the shock was palpable when mounting deaths extended the category of 'underlying vulnerability' further and further into the general population, as the 'otherness' of those at risk of the virus broke down, evidence accumulating that vulnerability was, in fact, in all of us, even the Prime Minister. Michael Winterbottom, director of a BBC drama about the pandemic, called this the 'discounting' of daily deaths: 'it's only people who are older', or 'it's only people with underlying conditions'.

The start of the pandemic was a time when, as a newspaper columnist wrote just after the first lockdown had got under way, 'the British are dying in "care" homes across the country without saying goodbye to their families ... The government said goodbye to goodbyes when it ordered care home providers to "stop all visits to residents from friends and family"' (Nick Cohen, *The Observer*, 5 April 2020).

Around this time we started clapping care workers on Thursday evenings. The same article continued:

> Few outsiders care about the care services ... Millions gather at their windows to applaud the frontline staff fighting the virus. The organisers say they are clapping 'healthcare workers, emergency services, armed services, delivery drivers, shop workers, teachers' and so on. Nowhere are home and residential care staff mentioned. So what, some might say. Banning visits is a necessary measure to contain the danger. It might be if the rest of the care system were not a lethal trap. Stories of the army finding the dead abandoned in their beds that make the hairs on the back of your neck stand on end have come out of Spanish old people's homes. We're not there, but no one should be surprised if the system buckled. It could barely cope before.
>
> (Nick Cohen, *The Observer*, 5 April 2020)

A week later, David Collins wrote: 'Joan, the mother of four children died in an isolation room, holding the hand of a carer as her daughter, Jenny, waved goodbye through a window' (*Sunday Times*, 12 April 2020).

Two years into the pandemic, the situation continued as a new strain of Covid, called Omicron, threatened already threadbare staffing levels, and many homes were refusing to allow visitors. At the time, the Care Quality Commission received 54 reports, as Omicron hit, of blanket bans on visiting at care homes. MP Liz Savile Roberts told fellow MPs she feared separation from her mother, who had dementia, when she moved from hospital into a nursing home. She said, 'the human rights of disabled people, sick people and the elderly are not Fairweather Luxuries, and everyone with dementia, wherever they live, has the right to care from a family member' (quoted by Emily Duggan, *Sunday Times*, 19 December 2021).

These articles were all written during the pandemic. And sure enough, after a while, we did start to 'clap for carers' too. Matt Hancock, then secretary of state for health, claimed that we had 'placed a protective ring' around care homes. Well, how did we do in protecting the vulnerable older adults being looked after in our care sector? At the time, we did not count this figure in a meaningful way, as deaths were not included in the government's official figures if the deceased had not been tested for the disease. David Collins wrote: 'the Office for National Statistics (ONS) reports that 2,489 people have died in care homes this year up to March 27 in England and Wales, but it counts only 20 of them as Covid-19 deaths' (*Sunday Times*, 12 April 2020).

What were the final figures? Did we stem the tide of death, with our draconian restrictions, which kept families exiled and absent from their loved ones in care? The answer is that the final tally was deaths of more than 41,000 residents with Covid in the first two waves of the pandemic. It was made worse, in the first wave, by the fact that infected patients were discharged from hospitals into care homes, causing outbreaks to race through the homes. Eventually, the Covid Enquiry began to report, and more evidence emerged which confirmed the reports that were coming out in the press at the time. For example, the Covid Enquiry released an email from the deputy chief medical officer sent in March 2020, as Covid was unfolding, in which she wrote:

> The reality will be that we will need to discharge Covid-19 positive patients into residential care settings ... The numbers of people with disease will rise sharply within a fairly short timeframe and ... I recognise that families and care homes will not welcome this in the initial phase.
>
> (*The Observer*, 3 December 2023)

The underlying attitudes behind this policy were laid bare in the diary of the chief scientific adviser at the time, Sir Patrick Vallance, also revealed by the Covid Enquiry. In his entry for October 2020, he noted: 'PM meeting – begins to argue for letting it all rip. Saying yes, there will be more casualties but so be it – "they have had a good innings ..." Most people who die have reached their time anyway' (*The Observer*, 3 December 2023). As Naomi Fulop of the organisation Covid-19 Bereaved Families for Justice pointed out:

> comments [from the then Prime Minister] such as that people dying have 'had their innings' [are] incredibly painful. One of the KCs [at the Covid Inquiry] called them shamefully ageist comments, which is what they are ... He's talking about my mother and thousands of other people who died before their time and in an awful context.
> (Naomi Fulop, *The Guardian*, 19 December 2023)

Many years ago, Simone de Beauvoir nailed this idea of 'having had one's innings', which in recent history seems to have had currency as a justification for actions taken during Covid. In her searing account of her mother's death, she wrote:

> *He is certainly at an age to die* ... I too made use of this cliché ... But it is not true. You do not die from being born, nor from having lived, nor from old age. You die from *something* ... All men must die but for every man his death is an accident and ... an unjustifiable violation.
> (de Beauvoir 2023 [1964], p. 111)

There are three essential aspects of the government response to Covid that reveal underlying attitudes to older people, and I believe they have not been sufficiently reported nor become part of national discussion.

At the start of the pandemic, older people were 'triaged' out of access to intensive care – unnecessarily, in terms of the resource demands on intensive care, as it turned out. Although never formally published, an age-based 'triage tool' was circulated to many NHS Trusts at the start of the pandemic which gave instructions that, in the event of the NHS being overwhelmed, patients over 80 should be denied access to intensive care. According to a report in the *Sunday Times* (Insight Team, 25 October 2020), in several hospitals this 'triage tool' was used, and, according to the evidence of this report, many older people were excluded from life-saving treatment at this point in the pandemic. Testimony from doctors, which the *Sunday Times* reports, confirms the tool was used to prevent elderly patients blocking intensive care beds. Indeed, the *Sunday Times* team report data from the NHS showing that the proportion of over-60s with coronavirus who received intensive care halved between the middle of March and the end of April 2020 as the pressure increased on hospitals. According to this analysis, 'Ultimately thousands of frail and elderly people across Britain died at home without hospital treatment'. A senior figure from the organisation Age UK, Caroline Abrahams, is quoted as saying, 'older people were considered dispensable … The lack of empathy and humanity was chilling. It was ageism laid bare and it had tragic consequences' (*Sunday Times*, 25 October 2020).

Early in the pandemic, people with Covid were discharged into care homes. The government knew at the time about asymptomatic Covid, and yet knowingly transferred people without safeguards from hospital into care homes, where they spread the virus to other residents. This was despite care home providers being 'very, very clear right from the get-go that we couldn't take people unless they were tested' (Sam Monaghan, Chief executive of MHA, the largest care home provider, who attended a meeting of large care home providers on 12 March 2020). Michael Savage and James Tapper reported, 'Some 25,000 people were discharged to care homes between 17th March and 15th April 2020, and there is a widespread belief among social care workers and leaders that this allowed the virus into care homes' (*The Observer*, 30 May 2021).

The High Court subsequently ruled that this policy had been illegal because the government failed to take account of the risk to elderly and vulnerable residents from non-symptomatic transmission, which had been highlighted by Sir Patrick Vallance in a radio interview as early as 13 March 2020. This news item on the High Court ruling that the Government had acted illegally was barely reported at the time it came out in Spring 2022.

The human rights of older adults in residential care were violated with the deprivation of visits in care homes. This continued not just in the initial phase of the pandemic, but, though the policy position shifted, in practice, over a period of nearly two years. And, on this last point, the consequences of the government's initial position that lockdown for care homes meant that family members could not visit, condemned many – probably an unknown number – to live out their last days, and to die, without being with their family.

Even one such death, if you try to imagine it, is one too many. There have been many deaths like this, and they were not even counted during the first months of the pandemic. If you think of this, and remember that older people were, in some cases, selectively denied intensive care on account of their age; that the government pursued the policy of transferring patients with Covid from hospital into care homes without the necessary safeguards – and that all of this took place when we knew that Covid was a disease which kills older people most of all, then it becomes clear that it adds up to a deadly enactment, at a societal level, of our hatred of old age. It is this which, ultimately, made death traps of our care homes during the pandemic. A familiar hatred enacted in a new way, for new times.

Perhaps I need to pause here for a moment, and answer the question: what do I mean by saying that, as a society, we hate old age and vulnerability? I think we can see this hatred refracted back to us in myriad ways, in our society's handling of ageing and our treatment of the elderly – and we can understand it, from a psychoanalytic perspective, as shall be explored in these pages. Our difficulty in facing our own future, as represented by the old and frail, has, in our recent history, made ghettos of places in which the elderly and the vulnerable are housed. In the days when I first started working as a psychologist there were psychogeriatric wards and so-called 'back wards' in the large asylums, where the 'warehousing' of older people with dementia created an environment of 'lost meaning' – a malignant mirroring of dementia in the system of care. Perhaps the same unconscious processes which produced such situations have now been enacted in a 'pandemic genocide' of older adults which has gone almost unnoticed: suffering and death which took place behind closed doors and out of sight, at the supposed civilised heart of our democracy, yet barely even newsworthy. This 'blind eye' that, as a society, we have largely turned to what happened is, I believe, an example of the quiet deployment of our hatred of, and wish to wipe out knowledge of, these painful realities of ageing and death. For if we see them, we are faced with stark evidence of our own frailty, vulnerability, and mortality.

In July 2022, Covid deaths reached 200,000. The author and broadcaster Michael Rosen wrote:

> 200,000 deaths is a lot of death for all of us to cope with ... the deaths have happened not in a public, shared way, in some horrific act of war ... [and so] it has become easier to tidy it away. The burden of the national and social trauma is being carried by us in our families and personal relationships ... I ask myself, did the virus get into my lungs at home? ... Or in the BBC Today programme studio talking about why I thought an unpleasant attitude was emerging that suggested that if old people got Covid and died it mattered less than if young people got it? ... One famous journalist reassured me that she knew I had been ill, 'but', she added, 'you are 74'. That 'but' is doing a lot of work. What's 'but' about being 74? Are my days less valid than her days, I ask myself. What kind of Social Contract do we have with each other in which I can be dispensable because I'm 74?
>
> (Michael Rosen, *The Guardian*, 16 July 2022)

This is, indeed, a vital question for us: what kind of social contract do we have in our society, where a youth culture prevails, and yet, like most Western societies, our population is ageing? Underpinning this, as shall be discussed as you read on, is the issue of what kind of psychological relationship we have with our own ageing selves. In the following chapters of this book, I am going to be thinking, from a psychoanalytic point of view, about what I have termed the 'developmental challenges' of late life and the anxieties these evoke for us, in prospect, throughout our lives. How hard it can be to bear the emotional demands of ageing! This is a central theme which is interwoven throughout this book. As a guide to what's ahead, below is a summary of each of the chapters that follow.

Chapter 1: Ageing in Body and Mind: The Challenges of Living a Long Life

As a society we are living longer lives – but the rate of human ageing has not changed in thousands of years. This means that we are all likely to inhabit ageing bodies and experience age-related illness and deterioration – and indeed this is happening on a scale unprecedented in previous generations. The chapter draws upon psychoanalytic developmental models to understand the early anxieties which may re-emerge for couples and individuals under the weight of the challenges of age-related changes to body and mind. Using case examples, it highlights the indivisibility of psyche and soma which is thrown into relief by the vicissitudes of age-related decline that is now being endured as a commonplace, as societies around the world become older. As with other chapters in the book, the emphasis is upon what may help people to endure such painful losses, highlighting the importance of being accompanied, internally and externally, through the 'journey' of late life and dying.

Chapter 2: Intimacy and Sexuality in Later Life

Age-related changes in sexual functioning are one of the key losses that we must bear in later life. In this chapter, the challenge of sustaining intimacy is linked to the capacity to face such losses – and others, such as the loss of the structures which may have helped to support our relationship earlier on, such as work and other features of the social environment. Case examples are explored, of couples whose intimate lives are affected by psychosexual difficulties, and where their capacity to work through these problems is impaired by deeper anxieties about intimacy. The chapter explores Oedipal conflicts at this stage of life, and draws upon poetry, Shakespeare's *King Lear*, and newspaper articles, to explore factors which support, and those which inhibit, the sustaining of intimacy in old age.

Chapter 3: Another Country? Migration and Internal Dislocation in Old Age

Dislocation is part of the history of psychoanalysis, as many of the first generation of analysts were refugees from Europe. This chapter draws parallels between the experience of the migrant and the internal experience of dislocation consequent on ageing itself – where psychically, if not geographically, one might find oneself in a foreign land. This chapter develops the concept of 'internal migration' – a defensive withdrawal to a state of psychic retreat and the phantasy of a 'timeless' world – when faced with the losses brought by the passage of time. Through clinical examples and poetry, the chapter highlights how damaging this can be – increasing isolation and loneliness and putting out of reach the good objects (internal, and external) which are needed to help navigate the challenges of this stage of life.

Chapter 4: Thinking about the Experience of Dementia: The Importance of the Unconscious Mind

This chapter explores the difficulty of learning about, and comprehending, the experience of dementia – highlighting the importance of considering unconscious processes in the individual with dementia and in their relationships with others, including in care settings. It is a profound challenge for us to think about what it may be like for a person to move into a world of encroaching incomprehension, and this chapter draws upon conversations with people who have dementia, as well as research carried out by the author which illustrate different levels of awareness, even in people at advanced stages of the disease who may not be thought to have conscious insight into their illness. The chapter discusses the importance of exploring meaning in dementia and, as part of this, considers the experiences of people living with the illness and their carers including those in the professional care setting. It concludes with a summary of recommendations for those who are looking after people with dementia.

Chapter 5: The Fragile Thread of Connection: Living as a Couple with Dementia

In focusing on the importance of the subjective experience of the couple who are living with dementia, this chapter complements the previous one. Drawing on findings from developmental and attachment-based research and linking these with psychoanalytic models, it explores the relationship opportunities, and challenges, of living with a partner who has dementia. Using case examples which are explored in depth, the chapter takes its discussion of the issues, which were initially discussed from a theoretical and research perspective, into the lived experience of couples with dementia. It explores what matters in dementia care – in particular, the importance of emotional contact and containment – and considers how hard it can be to sustain this. Overall, the chapter discusses how we might understand the emotional supports that are needed to sustain relationships and to hold people in their familiar relational context, and so maintain the resilience of couples and families who are living with the illness.

Chapter 6: Working Psychotherapeutically with Couples Who Are Living with Dementia

This describes an approach to working psychotherapeutically with couples who are living with dementia which has been developed by the author. This seeks to assist emotional contact, communication and understanding between partners in couples living with the illness (factors explored in the previous chapter as being of crucial importance). This chapter puts the voices of couples with dementia at its centre, exploring the experiences of both partners and looking at how they navigate the diagnosis and the changes in their relationship as dementia progresses. It also gives an account of the development of an intervention for such couples which is grounded in their everyday experiences, that is continuing to be developed at Tavistock Relationships.

Chapter 7: At Home in a Home? Institutional Care and the 'Unheimlich'

This chapter explores the issue of going into residential or institutional care, beginning with an exploration of the question of what it means to feel 'at home'. It uses Freud's concept of the 'Unheimlich' to look at this, discussing how family members of people with illnesses such as stroke or other acquired brain damage, may find themselves in a situation which has qualities of Freud's 'Uncanny' – where their loved one is still as they were in some respects, but oscillating with strangeness and a sense of 'death in life'. Significant numbers of people with such conditions eventually move into institutional care. The context of such care might be said to contain the ambiguity of the 'Unheimlich' – where 'going into *a* home' is predicated on a displacement *from* home and the familiarity of home, which can hold so much of personal identity, may be lost. Using case examples and an account of an observational study of a care home setting, the chapter looks at factors which might help to enable people to feel 'at home' in such an institutional home.

Chapter 8: Dying and Assisted Death

This takes up the theme of earlier chapters which discuss illness and death – focusing on the experience of approaching death and of choosing an assisted death. It begins with clinical material from an elderly patient whose body was deteriorated, but whose mind was very much alive, and where the psychotherapeutic work often focused on his anxieties about death. Then, the chapter moves into a discussion of the legal position of assisted death, and the current situation where such deaths are 'exported to Switzerland'. Much of the chapter centres on a closely written account of an assisted death. The aim in rendering this is to highlight key issues in the debate. In particular, the current policy position in the UK and in many other countries, which, in criminalising family members who assist such a death, drives people to make the journey to Switzerland while they are still well enough to do so. This means that the assisted death happens earlier than it might otherwise. This changes the psychic situation from one where death is more obviously a release from suffering, adding the emotional burden that the assisted death, which happens prematurely, more resembles an assisted suicide. The emotional consequences of this for families is discussed, offering a new inflection in the argument for legalising assisted death: a case for bringing assisted death home, so to speak, rather than 'exporting' it, so that people can live for as long as they feel able to, and die at home, not abroad.

References

de Beauvoir, S. (1965). What Can Literature Do? In Y. Buin (ed.), *Que peut la littérature?* Union Générale d'Éditions.
de Beauvoir, S. (1972). *Old Age*. Penguin.
de Beauvoir, S. (2023 [1964]). *A Very Easy Death*. Fitzcarraldo Editions.
Milne, A. A. (2024 [1927]). *Now We Are Six*. Farshore.

Chapter 1

Ageing in Body and Mind
The Challenges of Living a Long Life

People are living longer, our populations are ageing, many of us now likely to reach an age that would have been considered very old a generation ago. Half of all of those born after 2007 can expect to live to over 100, and as one newspaper headline put it: 'Those who are 60 now have the life of a 40-year-old from a century ago.' And there is no doubt that this extra time is a great opportunity – who has not looked at pictures of our parents or grandparents and said, 'my goodness they look ancient', when they were still at an age that would not now be considered old. However, as I shall discuss, this 'bonus time' faces us more than ever with the truth of Freud's dictum that the 'ego is first and foremost a body ego' and the economic and psychological consequences of this now confront us both as a society, and at the level of the individual, the couple and family on a scale never seen before. In Britain, for example, between 2010 and 2030 the number of people aged over 65 will increase by more than 50 per cent and the number of older people with disability or chronic illness by a similar proportion and as a result, our National Health Service will face a huge shortfall in its annual budget (Ince 2014).

The wish to extend life and defeat death may be, for the most part, a universal aspect of the human condition, faced as we are with the prospect of mortality. Medical science has been successful at pushing the limits of our life span, but the rate of human ageing has not changed in thousands of years. In Greek mythology, the god Eos asked Zeus for the gift of immortality for her lover Tithonus, but, so the myth goes, she forgot to ask for eternal youth as well. Tithonus was immortal – but pretty soon he was no longer youthful, and his years of immortality stretched out in endless ageing. Without eternal youth, our increased longevity presents us with psychological challenges, such as how to tolerate the losses of our physical and mental functioning, to which we shall be increasingly exposed the longer our lives go on.

This situation is not unique to our time. Freud himself was given a reprieve by life-saving surgery in 1923, and despite chronic pain he made creative use of his extra years. The painter Matisse is another famous example, saved by surgery, his physical disablement giving birth to new developments in his art in his last years. These men made good use of their 'bonus time'. Their

DOI: 10.4324/9781032636498-1

extra years are now a commonplace experience for many of us. Given this, greater understanding of the psychological factors likely to enable us to continue engaging creatively is very important – what helps to allow us to sustain and inhabit our longer lives? What are the developmental and anti-developmental factors that we need to understand to navigate this landscape of later life?

To consider these questions, I will draw on a developmental model, in which early anxieties and defences, and the failures and achievements of our earliest years, are seen as very relevant to understanding how these challenges of later life will be negotiated. Of course, within psychoanalysis there are different ways of thinking about early life and its significance for our development. I shall draw particularly upon Klein's notion of 'developmental positions', which captures how psychic development is not seen as static, never fully achieved, and that we oscillate between these positions throughout our lives, particularly under times of pressure, such as can present in old age. Klein's 'paranoid-schizoid'[1] and 'depressive'[2] positions are constellations of anxieties, defences, object relationships and other feelings – and they provide a useful framework for considering how one position or another might be dominant at any particular time. As I shall discuss, for some people, there may have been an equilibrium established earlier in their lives that doesn't hold under the weight of the difficulties of later life, in which early and more primitive anxieties may re-emerge, and which may expose vulnerabilities and fault lines which are the legacy of earlier times.

The Resurgence of the Body in Old Age

After a more silent period for many in younger adulthood, in old age the body asserts itself again and in later life this becomes inescapable. The novelist Penelope Lively writes from her own experience:

> Doctors' surgeries and hospital waiting rooms are well stocked with those over sixty-five; it is the old and the young who demand most attention. On a trip to [hospital] … a couple of years ago my companions in the waiting room were seven elderly men and women, and three mothers with babies or toddlers, all of us supervised by a stern-faced security man in case we started causing trouble … You get used to diminishment, to a body that is stalled, an impediment … you have to come to terms with a different incarnation.
> (Lively 2014, pp. 38–39)

The facts of our limited time on earth face us, perhaps more than anything, through the experience of our bodies. The imprint of ageing is on the physical body and the impact of this and its impingement upon the mind is signified by physical changes. Living longer, we are exposed more to the reality of physical ageing, to age-related illness and conditions such as dementia. Older couples are faced with ageing in the mirror of their partner's physical changes and are confronted with the prospect of losing control over their bodies and with death, and these existential issues are signalled in the everyday difficulties the couple may start to face in their daily lives. How we adjust to this and find an acceptance which is enough in accord with reality is crucial– and in the examples of some people, we can see a picture of hope – of later life as a time of development – of new riches, perhaps. Yet for others, there can be a claustrophobic quality of being trapped, or in flight from these pressing realities of age and what it augurs.

Awareness of Death

How can we be aware of transience in a way which enhances our capacity to live, rather than filling us with despair or distancing us from immersing ourselves in life while we have it? Freud, recalling the old adage *If you want peace, get ready for war*, suggests changing it to: *If you want to be alive, get ready for death* (De Masi 2004, p. 132). Yet how difficult it is for us to be aware of this, of our existence in time, to be in a state of mind where knowledge of the fact of our death shapes our perception of time passing – this is a developmental achievement. But for some, the fact of mortality may be impossible to bear, and the anxieties of this stage of life can bring a more deadly state of depression or psychic retreat[3] from the reality of time passing, into a timeless state – where death is effaced, leaving the person without internal good objects to support them and therefore without the resources for facing life, or death, and I shall return to this in the clinical case material which follows.

For Freud, the unconscious believes it is immortal – we cannot represent our non-existence in our minds and if we imagine death, we are present as spectators at our own funeral. Yet, as Money-Kyrle (1971) points out, we are confronted in the everyday losses that make up our lives with the fact of our finitude, with the inevitability of the loss of our objects, and ourselves. To my mind, these lines from Wallace Stevens's poem 'The Plain Sense of Things' convey something of the attempt to put into words our imagined non-existence:

> It is as if
> We had come to an end of the imagination ...
> Yet the absence of the imagination had
> Itself to be imagined. The great pond,
> The plain sense of it, without reflections, leaves,
> Mud, water like dirty glass, expressing silence ...
> (Stevens 1954, p. 503)

De Masi (2004) asks, how can we make death thinkable when it is both an unthinkable and yet also a disquieting presence in our minds? And here, I suggest, we need to include ageing itself, the embodied experience of time passing which is about loss and diminution of functioning – not only facing death, but the decline of functioning which contains the prospect of death within it. Death is gradual; as one of my patient's said, 'it isn't just switching off the light ... you see death in the little things you can't do anymore, that are lost'.

Return of Early Anxieties

In many ways, the infant you once were, you will always be, and this is as true of the older person at the end of life as it is of them in younger days – and this truth may be particularly heightened, as early anxieties can be rekindled at the end of life. T. S. Eliot wrote: 'In my beginning is my end' (Eliot 1944, p. 13) – birth and death are coupled. In late life we may have a return of our most primitive anxieties of the dissolution or fragmentation of the self – the actual threats of old age such as dementia, giving very real, external confirmation, of such core underlying fears.

From a psychoanalytic point of view, while there are of course differences between schools, there is perhaps a consensus on the importance of the infant's early vulnerability and anxieties, and that the mother's response can have crucial long-term implications for development. For Klein, the infant is born with a terror of annihilation, while for Winnicott babies who experience significant environmental failure early on then carry within them through life the experience of 'the agony of disintegration. They know what it is like to be dropped, to fall forever' (Winnicott 1969, pp. 259–260). In infancy, such terror of annihilation or disintegration was based on the infant's primitive state of physical and psychological vulnerability and for some people late life can bring a new iteration of such anxieties. While there are differences in these psychoanalytic approaches, perhaps what unites them is the understanding that what is important, in terms of the capacity of the mind to encompass this situation in old age, is how such anxieties were contained originally, in infancy. Where there have been early difficulties in dependency relationships, the threat of vulnerability and dependency in later life can be felt as a trauma to be avoided at all costs. The point here is that this is a trauma that has already happened in infancy, with the crucial difference that the infant is growing and developing with the potential for new experiences to repair things, whereas for the older person, the trajectory now is towards actual death. The question, then, is what scope is there for development in late life and I shall return to this issue in the clinical discussions which follow.

Analysts such as Money-Kyrle (1971) and McDougall (1986) include ageing and death as fundamental facts of life. As McDougall puts it:

How do we manage to bind the wounds to our narcissistic integrity caused by external realities such as the fact of ageing and finally the inevitability of death?' She adds, 'most of us manage to make unstable adjustment to these realities but there is little doubt that ... in our unconscious fantasies we are all omnipotent ... eternally young and immortal.

(McDougall 1986, p. 9)

How such 'facts of life' are negotiated is driven by the internal legacy of our earlier development. The challenges of later life may elicit powerful infantile anxieties and how these are experienced will depend on previously achieved developments, and here again I shall turn to Klein's notion of 'depressive position' functioning, which crucially includes the capacity to mourn. Where such developmental achievement has been possible, and such states of mind are accessible, then there will be the possibility for more internal reparation,[4] for grieving of the losses the couple are faced with – although the limits of time remaining, and the weight of loss that some must bear in old age, may test such capacities severely. Where paranoid schizoid states dominate, then the prospect of facing death and the end of life will be predominantly persecutory, with a sense of failure, of isolation and of being subject to demons. An example of this is Dickens's character of Scrooge, who, in his nightmares, gives us a picture of one's legacy being a torturing guilt and persecution, of Old Testament judgement and damnation.

Thinking again of the illnesses of old age, such as dementia, where there is the threat or actuality of fragmentation of the mind and body, what I have described is how this may be close to unconscious anxieties of fragmentation that have always been part of the internal world. The aged, declining body is a reality. We are all gripped by destructive drives, and when the body as an object of projection really is deteriorated and damaged, then inside and outside, inner phantasy and external reality may converge. This can cause particular problems, making mentalising, processing of feelings, and containment of destructiveness, more difficult- and can be felt as a claustrophobic sense of being trapped with a damaged object – projected into the body – which one has attacked and damaged and which retaliates with persecuting punishment and threats to existence.

I am now going to describe case examples which convey how the experience of illness and deterioration of the body in old age affects the people concerned, whose varying capacities to contain their feelings and to mourn the losses they are faced with, shape the way in which this phase of their lives unfolds. First, I will give an example of such a claustrophobic encounter for a couple with the reality of their mutual deterioration leading to a breaking down of their fragile equilibrium, increased cycles of projection, and the loss of capacity for containment in the psychiatric team around them.

This couple and the problems of the psychiatric team trying to look after them were brought to me for supervision. They had long-standing difficulties – but a more or less stable equilibrium had been maintained until the point at which there was physical deterioration and vulnerability in both. His brain operation and her operation and fitting of a stoma bag, which happened almost at the same time, led to an increased sense of claustrophobia at home. They showed great difficulty in tolerating close physical proximity – and expressed hatred and disgust at the changes in the other partner. It seemed to be literally a case of 'keep the shit away from me'. Her intense humiliation and rage when, in the heat of one of their rows, which were escalating, he threw her stoma bag out of the window. They tried demarcation areas at home – creating separate domestic zones in the house, his space or hers – her kitchen, separate bathrooms – but this did not work. One was still felt to be invading the other's space – he comes into her kitchen; she invades his bathroom. It was a picture of increasingly volatile and escalating rows, of the experience of claustrophobic invasion, with aggression as a response – which further escalated the feeling of intrusion, takeover and sense of dangerousness of the situation. Against this background, she put pressure on the team, demanding that the consultant should change her husband in this way or that way, and if he didn't prescribe the medication she wanted, she would ring up every day. It was very difficult for the psychiatric team to find any way of thinking or containment in the face of this barrage. As she felt more persecuted and out of control of her body, and her mind – and the disequilibrium between them, and the cycle of projections intensified – the team felt increasingly controlled and unable to function with separate, thinking minds themselves. 'We can't carry on like this' the psychiatrist said. She could have been speaking the words of the wife, who said, 'I can't live with him anymore' and began a campaign to have her husband admitted to a care home. Yet, he did not need looking after in a home, the team felt, and initially they resisted. However, the rows were escalating more, and eventually, the team decided that the best thing was to help them separate, as they saw it, by admitting him to a home.

As the physical problems took hold, the couple intensified their projections into one another, trying to split off and deny these aspects of themselves, by attempting to effect a physical separation from one another in his move to the home. But what was apparent was the instability of this solution, which was an attempted getaway from parts of themselves that could not be disposed of in this way. The situation of the couple was one of claustro-agoraphobia – of being trapped by bodies that were frighteningly fallible, deteriorating and inescapable and which provoked hatred and projection, the need to get rid of these frightening and persecuting aspects of the self – literally evacuated, the stoma thrown out of the window.

Opening a 'window' of thought on such disturbing mental states is a difficult business, but containment, offering a receptive mind to try to take in and process such states of mind, can be very important in helping couples to negotiate the challenges of late life. In this example, what is also evident in the struggle that the psychiatric team experienced when faced with such powerful projections from this couple, is how difficult this can be. Perhaps these two factors: the importance of containment and the difficulty of sustaining a containing mind when faced with states of physical and psychic fragmentation are nowhere more apparent than in the emotional difficulties the couple may encounter when one partner has dementia, which I shall now discuss.

Dementia

Our awareness of the indivisibility of psyche and soma is thrown into relief by the threat of dementia, a condition where organic changes bring loss of mind. As our longevity increases, so the incidence of dementia rises – one in five people over eighty develop it and there have been predictions that in due course half of the population will develop dementia before they die. Statistically then, the odds are very high that at least one partner in a couple may develop dementia in late life.

What happens to such couples then, when one of the partners becomes ill with a deteriorating condition such as dementia? One pattern that can be observed is a 'negative loop of withdrawal', where the person with dementia becomes more anxious about 'getting it wrong', less able to keep up with verbal communication and withdraws. The partner without dementia often takes over more and more, compounding the disablement of their partner, both becoming more emotionally out of contact with one another. And there can be the additional problem of the loss of the couple's social world, which can amplify the isolation and the claustrophobic anxieties of the couple, as they are thrown back more upon one another, with diminished external contacts. One woman described how, as the dementia progressed, they had been shunned from the social life of friends:

> There is an unease and awkwardness about being with someone with Alzheimer's disease, and the people who come to visit with Martin and me has dwindled away to nothing ... People find it hard to understand that I am strongly connected to him ... Being wanted and supported as part of a couple is still relevant now – being recognised as linked. When I go out socially, people respond as though I am alone and don't recognise that I am part of this couple, that Martin is at home, that I have a bond with him.

Quinodoz (2014) describes the difficulty when such couples withdraw into psychic retreat, in refuge from paranoid schizoid and depressive anxieties, and shut themselves away, no longer in communication with outside, and emotional contact can also be lost between them. The claustrophobia of the situation can be palpable, and she writes of the need to open a window, to let air in from outside (Quinodoz 2014, p. 95). I would say that opening a window and 'letting in air' is to express, and have a receptive mind available to take in, both verbalised feelings as well as non-verbal projection, which in the case of dementia may increasingly replace language as the disease progresses. To hold on to communication and emotional meaning within the couple for as long as possible, and to this end, help can be needed, though there are few psychological interventions available for such couples. This approach is the essence of Living Together with Dementia, an intervention developed at Tavistock Relationships in London (see Chapter 6), which draws on psychoanalytic thinking and video-based approaches to pick up meaningful communications when they happen and to help the couple to find meaning in everyday things, with the aim of increasing understanding and emotional contact between partners.

One woman with dementia vividly conveyed the strain of just managing – having to attend to ordinary everyday things, to concentrate – on not falling, on remembering, holding things together, constantly fighting against loss, fragmentation of experience and encroaching disintegration. She told me how she has to work so hard day to day, moment by moment, to make sure she has everything, and then finds that her back-up drive for her laptop is lost. She looks everywhere, and then finds that her husband has found it and, worst of all, it is where it was supposed to have been. So the object is found, but she encounters memory loss – the fragmentation of her mind, of her functioning – which is letting her down, while she is working so hard to hold onto it. She feels rage towards him when he is in any way felt to be critical of her, when he echoes the self-criticism that is there in her own mind. Her husband feels he has to be very careful all of the time, walking on eggshells and, of course, he cannot maintain this. She feels shut out from the world of fast wit, and increasingly she is not part of that community of language in the same way anymore. At one session, she comments on a person on the train talking non-stop, and how she noticed the other person who was with them was shut out of the conversation. She feels shut out sometimes and also marvels at her husband's capacities, she says he seems to be doing things, thinking so fast. She told me that when he touches her softly, physical contact that comforts her, it feels different. He was on his laptop at breakfast, typing fast, so she got out her laptop, and as she put it, he got the message, shut his down, and pushed the lid down of her machine, touched her arm and engaged with her. She tells me that she wonders what sort of connection animals have, physically with one another, or trees with one another. Her displacement from the world of language is gradually happening more, and for now she can still express this and her awareness of her greater need for physical contact with him, for closeness …

And there is a sense that they can be closer now – he says they have more intimacy than was possible when they were younger. He describes how they are together, how they hold each other physically more now and his care for her, in other intimate ways, feels to him to be a way in which they can be closer than they were in their youth, that he can make it up to her, for his unavailability then. But things can also be more difficult between them – and some way into the work with them he is able to talk about his aggression towards her when he is feeling most frustrated. And his experience of being able to talk about this and have his feelings taken in within the therapy seems linked to the increasing recovery of more intimacy between them.

What is interesting is the capacity of this couple, including the partner with dementia, to be in touch with loss and to find ways of thinking about and tolerating such painful feelings. What I think is evident is how much capacity they both brought into the situation, in terms of their ability to mourn and hence to stay in some emotional contact with themselves and with each other. To what extent, as the pressure of the illness increases and capacities are lost, more persecuted states of mind may begin to dominate is unclear – but my clinical impression is that, to some degree at least, this depends on how much containment can be offered by the partner without dementia. If we think of the original model of containment for a moment (Bion 1962), what is entailed is the taking in, and processing of experience (in the original developmental model, the mother is doing this for the infant) and conveying back in some way, that understanding – so that unmanageable experience is rendered more digestible, and can be taken back in, in a modified form. The psychoanalyst Margot Waddell (2007) points out how windows of clarity, of a briefly more integrated state, may be opened for the person with dementia when emotional contact is made through finding some way, in words or action, of conveying that understanding to them.

But the point is that this can be very difficult. It is important to recognise the tremendous challenge facing the carer and not to idealise what is possible. This draws our attention to the importance of the state of mind of the carer partner and their need for support and containment. They may have other feelings towards the individual with dementia in their care, apart from compassionate ones, such as resentment or hatred and there may be a great need for help and containment with this. And yet, approaches to interventions generally do not address this more difficult area.

Towards More 'Containment' in the Couple Relationship

Those with personal experience of dementia may recognise the situation of coming up against concrete complaints that have a quality of perseveration which, as they go on, can be wearing and feel meaningless – things are going missing – or being taken, or broken into. For example, to return to the couple I described, the female partner complained in a repetitive way about losing what she called 'her valuables', her jewellery – and her husband found the relentless perseveration of the same complaint extremely frustrating, and tended to withdraw and disengage in response. Part of the work was to try to think about whether, alongside the real frustration of losing these actual objects, there may also be something else being communicated, that perhaps centred around the theme of the losses that they were facing together. After some time there were shifts, for example she started talking about the loss of her dreams: 'I miss my dreams, since the dementia, I don't remember my dreams anymore. They used to be so vivid and often I would write them down ... but now I can't catch hold of them.' There was a lessening of the sense of her being so gripped by the more concrete, repetitive complaints and a shift to a poignant expression of her feelings about the precious things she was losing. 'I can be feeling normal, and then I lose my jewellery ... and it's like the dementia crashing in ... it's the loss of my mind that I am seeing', she said. In parallel with this, her husband seemed to become more interested in thinking about what might be going on in his wife, to be curious about a possible meaning behind what could seem, on the face of it, to be meaningless accusations and complaints coming out of the blue. Whereas before these almost always provoked anger and frustration in him and a walling off response ('I've just got to block it out', 'she's driving me mad'), he seemed to be able to have more space at times to take in her distress, and to offer her reassurance. They began to cope with the complaints in various ways, setting a time limit in which they would look for the jewels together, which had a calming effect and finding Perspex boxes to enable her to see where her things were better. There was also more transparent communication about the loss of her capacities and the losses within the relationship. He spoke more of what he couldn't hold onto in her: 'She is the most precious thing to me and I'm frightened that soon I won't be able to find her again, even for short times.' I think that being able to know about his own loss, and having someone talk to him about this, allowed him to be more available to her experience of loss, to contain it better – 'I can't say it'll be alright, but I'll be alongside you, we'll go through it together', he said to her.

She responded, 'we are having a very open discussion now ... this is the antithesis of the dementia, which makes me feel so hemmed in ...' Interestingly, at this point in the work, I heard that she returned to reading novels – something she had not done since the diagnosis, but which had always been important to her. Perhaps this example reflects the difficulty for the couple of the loss of what is so precious, which is of a sense of meaning to their actions and conveys something of a recapturing of a meaningful narrative, if you like. In dementia, this may be fleeting and as the illness progresses, the person with dementia will be less able to do this, but if there can be kept alive a sense of the potential meaning behind behaviour or interactions, it is a reminder of the humanity of the other and helps to hold onto a sense of the personal – and this is important for the carer in the longer term, and for both partners in the couple, if emotional meaning can be held onto for as long as possible. My clinical experience has been that what is so crucial, even in states of cognitive loss and deterioration, as in dementia, where language is being lost and projection may increasingly replace verbal communication, is the presence of another mind to take in, to accompany. People need to be met, emotionally, by another mind – and helped to make their experience thinkable.

Loss of the Couple in Old Age

Many people in late life are no longer in couple relationships, often as a consequence of divorce or the death of their partner, and loneliness and depression are a common experience. Indeed, the incidence of loneliness in old age is an increasingly recognised problem

Perhaps the most profound loss in old age may be of a partner. Needless to say, how difficult to lose someone with whom you may have spent a lifetime. For some people, after such a loss, a strong internal sense of the presence of their partner may be retained. The novelist Penelope Lively writes of how her husband who has died remains a presence inside her, an inner companion: 'Jack is nearly always present in my dreams. It is twelve years since he died, but at night he returns, not always recognizably himself, but a shadowy dream companion figure that I always know to be him' (Lively 2014, p. 44). But for others, there can be an experience of feeling cut off, without inner supports – and this state of mind may be very difficult to endure, linked to depression and withdrawal in old age, and I shall explore this in the case example which follows.

In the situation where there has been a prevalence of unresolved grief and ambivalence and within the relationship where the projective system has been more rigid and inflexible, with the loss of the partner there may be more likelihood of experiencing profound loneliness and depression, and greater difficulty in mourning and in reparative processes emerging, which would otherwise afford more of a sense of restoration of the other in the internal world, of their being experienced as an inner companion, as Lively puts it. In the following example, I shall discuss work with an individual whose husband had died a few years before she came for help, and where the 'ghost of the couple' was an important feature of the work with her.

I shall describe the case of a 90-year-old woman which I think illustrates the situation of a psychic retreat into a state of 'timelessness', which can be encountered in patients of any age, but which may become amplified as a response to facing the end of life and the limits of time remaining, signifying a retreat from the reality of loss, and the vulnerabilities of the end of life and death. The work with this patient involved helping her to bear the mental pain of the limitations of time and her underlying anxiety about the state of her objects, and describes her gradual emergence out of her state of timelessness to bear more the reality of loss and guilt, becoming more in touch with her internal and external objects and more able to face the limits of the reparation that was possible at this point in her life.

She had outlived her husband by several years. They had had a difficult marriage, and since his death she had withdrawn into a depressed state of mind. While I was not doing couple therapy 'beyond the grave', many will be familiar with the notion of working with the individual, but with the couple in mind. Such work with people at this point in life, where the partner has died, has particular dimensions to it, where the scope for effecting change in the actual, external relationship is gone and there can be a struggle with the question, 'Is it too late?' The hope that may be part of therapeutic work with younger patients is that inner reparation leads to changes in current relationships, with an adult partner, with children. For the therapist working with older people where the partner has died, one has the 'ghost of the relationship' in the room, which cannot be repaired in actuality, though perhaps may be in mind.

As she had encountered more and more physical difficulties, she had felt increasingly isolated and lonely, though had tried to continue with her academic work, which she was struggling to sustain. The state of her body, and her mind, were hard to bear: 'blood pressure, pain and swelling in my feet and hands, the pain in my neck – I am a mess ... everything is fragmenting.' She was out of contact with the people around her who could have provided some emotional companionship and spent a lot of time berating herself for having 'failed' in her marriage, and in other relationships. Such thoughts dominated her mind in a repetitive way and, as I came to understand, served to disallow any real thinking about the relationship she had had with her husband and her current situation with important people in her life. Lifelong internal accusations that she was not good enough and was failing had renewed purchase now, when things were not in reality working anymore, when her body was 'failing' her – and perhaps functioned protectively, defending against the reality of the changes in her body by converting this situation about which nothing could be done – a fact of life – into something familiar, a failing for which she was responsible and, by implication, could control. Maintaining the familiar state of recrimination perpetuated the belief that everything was in her gift, and I felt this was part of her retreat which kept her out of emotional contact with others, and with her own need and vulnerability. Although she felt persecuted by accusations of failure, these had an unchanging, repetitive quality which was very familiar to her and which I came to feel offered a 'psychic shelter' from other anxieties and fears. If she left this state of retreat, she would have to face the reality that she could not control her deteriorating body that was ageing, and this seemed to be linked to fears of disintegration and fragmentation. The timelessness of the internal criticism served to keep her away from facing the realities of where she was in her life; the limits of time remaining, real questions of how she wanted to spend the time that was left to her.

While in the sessions, I could feel I was 'drifting along' with her, I also began to feel uncomfortable, that she was running out of time – to see friends who were ill, to speak to her daughter, to spend time with her grandchildren. Yet, always, there was a refrain that these things were distractions from the real real task of focusing on her academic projects, and she pushed herself to work long hours. I came to understand that the omnipotent expectations on her body denied the reality of how compromised her functioning was, and her fears about how much worse it might become. She was often late for her sessions, acting as though nothing had happened, and in full flow at the end, as if with no awareness of the limits of time available. I found it difficult to tell her that the session was over, having to interrupt her abruptly – with the feeling that I was doing something callous and dislocating to her. I found myself worrying about her lack of urgency, and yet I felt that to say anything about this would be a cruel puncturing of her fragile state. I was told of other analysts she had seen a long time ago – these were famous names – leaving me feeling, what could I do? As time went on, I began to feel that I was in the position of being asked to carry her anxieties about the limits of time remaining, and of what could be repaired at this point in her life, the fear that to know about this, to emerge from the comforts of the 'timeless' state, would be a psychic disaster. My anxiety about how catastrophic it would be to put into words how she was self-destructively limiting the life she had now, seemed to reflect the fear that it would be impossible to bear the mental pain of knowing about this.

In terms of her earliest experience, I was told that her mother, who was struggling with a husband away at war and then deeply troubled upon his return, had put her in the care of her grandmother in her earliest months of life. Her early dependency relationships had been very difficult, and as I came to understand it, her contemporary terror of falling apart, which was brought close by her physical decline and the threat of worse to come, rekindled an early infantile terror of fragmentation. I came to think of her situation in the way Winnicott describes: the feared state of impending fragmentation was something that had already happened in the past, in her earliest life, consequent on failures of containment in her relationships with her primary objects. There was a sense of a 'narrowing of the gap' between the impinging realities of ageing, the sense that physically and mentally she was falling apart, and these underlying fears, which perhaps had 'waited in the wings' all her life. It seemed to me that this amplified the internal pressure on her to rise above her vulnerabilities and her dependency, to escape the terrors that these entailed – but at the same time, her mental and physical exhaustion made it increasingly difficult for her to sustain the harsh regime, the escape into solitary work, which she imposed on herself.

The feeling that it was 'too late' was very painful, glimpsed at moments when she did allow herself to be more in touch with the realities of the marriage she had had and how she was spending her time now, cutting herself off from people who were important in her life. Such moments tended to be fleeting, as she felt in touch with painful feelings of loss, and then retreated again. She would say to me, what is the point in coming here – you can't change any of these things. Indeed, I couldn't hold back time, could not take away the painful losses she was confronted with, nor change the past. I began to think that her preoccupation with how she was failing in her task of finishing her academic project might be a displacement of the reparative work which she neglected, but which I felt she was perhaps becoming more conscious of, and there were hints that she was starting to think about how she was neglecting her life that she could have available to her, particularly with her daughter and grandchildren. On one occasion, she hadn't gone to a family event, because, she said, she needed to work on her project. Yet though she had missed it, she hadn't then managed to get much work done and felt such a failure. Her response was to speak of how she had to work harder and shouldn't waste her time reading novels. I said that I thought she had been feeling bad that there was something which she was attending to, the preoccupation with her project, which was stopping her from attending to the life she had – with her daughter and granddaughters – and that, when she sees this, she feels terrible and punishes herself by stopping herself from having anything pleasurable, going back even more forcefully into her academic world. The difficulty was that she couldn't know about what she was doing without feeling tremendous pain and then returning to the persecutory state of mind again, going back into her retreat.

Gradually, she showed evidence of being aware of the significance of time lost. She started arriving on time and asked to increase the frequency of her sessions. As she began to be more in touch with the reality of the passage of time and the limits of time remaining, there was a poignant sense that each session, each gap between, could be the last. When she was ill, or caught cold, I had an acute awareness that this could be the illness that overtook her and she expressed this feeling – how each thing she decided not to do, may be her last chance to do it.

As the therapy went on, a sense of urgency became more apparent in the work, and there seemed to be an increasing pressure for her to repair things, alternating with her sense of helplessness at being able to fix herself, or her inner objects, which, as I have said, she managed by retreating into the state of 'timelessness'. Yet she conveyed to me the terror that she would run out of time and that this would happen before she had been able to sort things out in herself, before she had been able to put some order inside in relation to internal and external objects. And she brought accounts of people who had died before they were ready. As the 'timeless' feeling began to be moved away from, what was faced more fully were the limits of time left for repair, and in particular, the time that had been lost for the actual repair of the relationship with her husband. She conveyed the difficulty of bearing the pain of the fact that she couldn't, in reality, make things better with him, and that the man who may have helped her to bear the pain was not any longer there. But there was more of a sense of his being felt as an available presence in her mind, and there was less persecutory guilt – though this felt much sadder and more painful. She told me that she had started tending his grave, which had been left neglected and overgrown, and there were also signs of her beginning to look after her own body more – recognising her vulnerabilities and getting help where she could, for the things which could be improved.

At that point in the therapy there was a painful quality of sadness, as the possibility of more creative reparation began to emerge. She became in touch with a more mixed picture of her relationship with her husband. She told me that she had been looking at photographs of him and was reminded of when he was younger. It was like seeing a ghost of the man who had loved her, she said: 'I suppose, I can see the shadow of an earlier picture of him – and it is uncanny, sort of spooky.' And she told me that she had found old pictures of her and her father holding hands, seeming happy, and one where she was with her father and her mother, a picture of the family as intact. She began putting together a photograph album for herself, integrating pictures of her husband, herself, her daughter and her parents – and she gave one to her daughter, for her to hold onto for the future.

A little later in the work with her, she told me that she had been having very vivid dreams –where she was on a journey and she remembered that in the dream she had wondered why she had to be alone, why the others who were there couldn't come with her. She thought of *King Lear*; at the end of the play, the Duke of Kent says he must 'go on a journey', which is to his death. She added, 'I tend only to think of death as a release – but maybe there are anxieties about it – will I be in pain, will I suffer?' She told me that she wouldn't any longer be able to make the journey to see me in the wintertime, it would be too dark, and although there were practical ways around this, I thought that symbolically she was conveying how she wouldn't be with me at the end of her life, on her final journey. I thought that she was struggling with how to make the 'final journey' with a sense of not being totally alone, how to feel accompanied – in contact with her good objects. It felt that the journey in therapy with me had been to let go of the more persecuting state – so she wasn't stuck in her retreat, not totally alone – even though I would not be there with her at the end.

In a sense, she had spent a lifetime seeking to make reparation, working therapeutically with vulnerable people, taking on worthy causes. But this activity perhaps had evaded a more real reconciliation which contained an acceptance of what couldn't be repaired – reconciling herself more to the husband she had had, and the partner she had been, which allowed more recovery and restoration of the man who once had loved her and whom she had loved, before the relationship had become too damaged by their mutual attacks and withdrawal from one another. It felt that there had been an importance about capturing this before she died. Perhaps what had brought her to therapy, unconsciously at least, were thoughts of the 'midnight hour'. During the work, there was a softening and lessening of her tormented state, more capacity to grieve and to face losses, and a recovery of earlier pictures, particularly of her husband and of her father and mother, which felt to be significant in terms of her feeling that she had some inner companionship and was not totally alone in facing the end of her life.

Conclusion

What is unique to our times is the scale upon which we are faced with the problem and the opportunity of our longer lives. I have described some of the challenges that this can present. At a psychic level, living longer means more of us are exposed to age-related illness, bringing a new relationship to the body, which signifies the diminution and loss of capacity, and eventual death. De Masi (2004, p. 66) points out that the fear of death is 'irreducible' and working through persecutory anxieties is not going to do away with it, death being the ultimate expression of our human vulnerability. In the face of this, we all need our protections, and as Brearley (2005, p. 1497) says, perhaps all we can hope for 'is a balance between thick and thin skin, between destructiveness and reparation, between illusion and reality'. But there is a question of how the end of life can be 'good enough', and such restoration as can be possible, achieved, and I would add to this list the hope of being able to be accompanied, the struggle to keep an inner and external companionship with a good object.

The difficulty, then, is in defences that destroy good objects that are needed to help manage the challenges of this time and that can leave the person feeling abandoned with a sense of inner loneliness, whether or not they are actually alone. In couples, retreat, withdrawal, and loss of emotional contact is painful to witness, and the research indicates that the quality of our relationships at this point in life have profound, material consequences linked to rate of decline of illness and even mortality rates. The fragmentation of physical and mental states, which is threatened by age-related conditions such as dementia, gives 'corporeality' to primitive psychic phantasies of fragmentation and dissolution of the self. Unsurprisingly, in the face of these threats, people may withdraw into states of psychic retreat, depression, or psychotic decompensation. Defences which may have served well enough before may no longer hold up, and where there have been problems in dependency relationships earlier in life, failures of containment early on, there may be problems and defences can become amplified or break down, leading to more destructive states of mind taking a grip.

There is often a need for help to manage the losses of this period, which may bring the fear of worse changes to come. I have tried to highlight how, for the therapist working with people in late life, there might be pressures felt in the countertransference. We are faced with our limits in terms of what we can offer such patients therapeutically, and with the challenge of knowing about these limits without giving up in despair or becoming manic in what we do. It is difficult to tolerate close emotional contact with states of psychic or physical fragmentation and diminution in functioning and we are faced with our own mortality. This brings to mind again McDougall's words: 'in our unconscious fantasies we are all omnipotent ... eternally young and immortal' (McDougall 1986, p. 9). This work challenges such fantasies – and how difficult it can be then, to allow oneself to know about this situation of late life, of the limits of time remaining, without distancing oneself. It can be very difficult to hold onto this knowledge, while also retaining a sense of the possibility of psychic development that may still take place.

The first case example showed a primitive constellation of anxieties and defences that appeared to have broken down in the face of the difficulties the couple encountered in old age. It seemed that they struggled with powerful claustrophobic anxieties and there was massive projective identification within the couple and a sense of being hemmed in by a damaged internal object, represented in the experience of damage to somatic and psychic integrity which each partner projected into, and recoiled from, in the other. In the second case example, I felt that the picture of the couple was one where both partners' minds had been very developed with considerable emotional maturity, but where it was difficult to hold onto their capacities that were being so challenged by the dementia. Despite the fragmentation of psychic functioning attendant upon dementia, there was evidence of this couple's struggle to manage this, and to face the losses together – and at least for the moment, a sense of their trying to accompany one another through their experience. In the final case example, I focused upon more omnipotent defences: the retreat into timelessness as a reaction to the mental pain of vulnerability, loss and fragmentation.

If couples can be helped to emerge from the psychic restriction of internal retreat, or withdrawal, they may be able to mourn and recover more contact with good objects internally. And with each other, there may be less persecution and greater internal and external support for facing the 'final journey'. What is apparent here is the importance of containment– being helped to think, to process experience, to mourn losses – including grief for development that was not possible, life that hasn't been lived. What we might hope for is that the partners in such couples are not driven to retreat nor recoil from one another in the face of the losses and threats to psychic and somatic integrity in ageing, but are equipped instead with a tolerance that allows for contact and accompaniment through the process of late life and dying. These lines from a poem of Elaine Feinstein's come to mind:

> *Hold my hand*, you said in the hospital.
> ...
> *Hold my hand*, you said. *I feel*
> *I won't die while you are here.*
> You took my hand on our first aeroplane
> and in opera houses, or watching

> a video you wanted me to share.
> *Hold my hand,* you said. *I'll fall asleep*
> *And won't even notice you're not there.*
> (Feinstein 2007, p. 12)

I think this conveys the importance of feeling accompanied on that final journey. This behoves us – at both a social level, and at the level of the individual, couple, and family – to engage with the experience of ageing and the end of life. Quinodoz's 'window' needs to be opened – a window of thought – on this area of lived experience that we all face and yet which can be so hard for us to know about.

Notes

1. A state of mind in which splitting and projection dominate, along with a lack of separateness, feeling persecuted, and persecuting in relation to the other.
2. A more integrated state in which there is greater reflexiveness, separateness, and capacity to bear guilt and to mourn. See Klein (1957) for an expanded description of both the paranoid schizoid and depressive positions.
3. Psychic retreats (e.g. Steiner 1993) or 'pathological organisations' of the personality refer to tightly knit defences which function both (1) to enable people to avoid overwhelmingly persecutory and depressive anxieties by avoiding emotional contact with others and with internal and external anxiety, and (2) to provide a precarious psychic equilibrium that is achieved through the pathological impairment of a more responsive emotional self. Such 'retreats' are attempts to provide a new position that is at a remove from the normal fluctuations between the paranoid-schizoid and depressive positions.
4. Karl Abraham (1924) described the process of 'internal reparation' in normal grief, as part of the psychic reconstruction of the lost object inside the ego. The work of mourning is therefore about the stable re-introjection of the image and memory of the loved object within one's inner world. This is the only way in which the lost object, having re-established itself in the ego can be re-animated and experienced as alive. The internalisation of the lost object in the psychic world is a compensation for the real loss and it facilitates the working through of the pain and depressive anxieties.

References

Abraham, K. (1924). A Short Study of the Development of the Libido. In K. Abraham, *Selected Papers on Psychoanalysis.* Hogarth Press.
Bion, W. (1962). *Learning from Experience.* Heinemann.
Brearley, M. (2005). Review of the Book Making *Death Thinkable* by Franco De Masi. *International Journal of Psychoanalysis,* 86, 1493–1497.
De Masi, F. (2004). *Making Death Thinkable.* Free Association Books.
Eliot, T. S. (1944). East Coker. In T. S. Eliot, *Four Quartets.* Faber & Faber.
Feinstein, E. (2007). Hands. In E. Feinstein, *Talking to the Dead.* Carcanet Press.
Freud, S. (1923). The Ego and the Id and Other Works. In J. Strachey (ed. and trans.), *The Standard Edition of the Works of Sigmund Freud, Vol. 19.* Hogarth Press.

Ince, M. (2014). *Living with Dementia. Britain in 2015: Essential Research on the Issues that Matter.* ESRC.

Klein, M. (1957). *Envy and Gratitude and Other Works 1946–1963.* Hogarth Press.

Lively, P. (2014). *Ammonites and Leaping Fish: A Life in Time.* Penguin.

McDougall, J. (1986). *Theatres of the Mind: Illusion and Truth on the Psychoanalytic Stage.* Free Association Books.

Money-Kyrle, R. (1971). The Aim of Psychoanalysis. *International Journal of Psychoanalysis,* 61, 153–160.

Steiner, G. (1993). *Psychic Retreats: Pathological Organisations in Psychotic, Neurotic and Borderline Patients.* Routledge.

Quinodoz, D. (2014). Film Essay: Amour. *International Journal of Psychoanalysis,* 95, 375–383.

Stevens, W. (1954). The Plain Sense of Things. In W. Stevens, *Selected Poems.* New York: Alfred A. Knopf.

Waddell, M. (2007). Only Connect – the Links between Early and Later Life. In R. Davenhill (ed.), *Looking Into Later Life. A Psychoanalytic Approach to Depression and Dementia in Old Age.* Karnac Books.

Winnicott, D. W. (1969). The Mother–Infant Experience of Mutuality. In E. J. Anthony and T. Benedek (eds), *Parenthood: Its Psychology and Psychopathology.* Little, Brown & Co.

Chapter 2

Intimacy and Sexuality in Later Life

From a train window I spotted an advertising hoarding for life insurance that showed a face made up of two halves. On one side it was youthful, and on the other it was aged. I thought that this captured something essential about a psychoanalytic view of old age – the sense of the older and younger faces so closely linked, the older one containing the stamp of the younger one. It is, of course, a developmental model, and sexuality and its vicissitudes are a central part of that development. What, then, of the changing face of sexuality as we get older? When thinking about this topic we need a complex view of sexuality, linked to our psychic development and to the development of our capacity for sustained intimacy with other people – something that has been a central concern of psychoanalysis since the inception of Freud's revolutionary thinking, which began with sexuality, and with infantile sexuality in particular, more than a century ago. The question I want to address in this chapter is whether sexuality undergoes particular developmental pressures in later life.

Louis Noirot, a French physician, observed in 1873 that 'in old age, like our hair, our desires should wither' (quoted in Stearns 1979, p. 243). Ruth Rendell, a novelist then aged 76, said in an interview published in *The Guardian* (16 September 2006): 'With age a lot of things go that one loved. Sex, of course, but I think its departure is proper and natural and not to be mourned.' Contrast this with a poem written by Thomas Hardy when he was an old man, which conveys the persistence of sexual longing in later life:

> I look into my glass
> And view my wasting skin
> And say, 'Would God it came to pass
> My heart had shrunk as thin!'
>
> For then, I, undistrest
> By hearts grown cold to me,
> Could lonely wait my endless rest
> With equanimity.

But time, to make me grieve,
Part steals, lets part abide;
And shakes this fragile frame at eve
With throbbings of noontide.

Changes Associated with Ageing

As ever, in regard to matters related to ageing, Freud himself was pessimistic. In a letter to Lou Andreas-Salomé, dated 10 May 1925, he wrote:

> As for me, I no longer want to ardently enough. A coat of indifference is slowly creeping around me. It is a natural development, a way of beginning to grow inorganic. The 'detachment of old age' I think it is called. It must be connected with a decisive turn in the relationship of the two instincts postulated by me. The change taking place is perhaps not very noticeable; everything is as interesting as it was before... but some kind of resonance is lacking; unmusical as I am, I imagine the difference to be something like using the pedal or not.
> (Freud et al. 1978, p. 237)

Freud confided quite a lot in his letters to her about his feelings about his ageing and the physical illness that accompanied it. For example, when he wrote to her to acknowledge her congratulations on his 75th birthday, he commented that he found it wonderful that she and her husband could still enjoy the sun. He added: 'But with me, the grumpiness of old age has moved in, the complete disillusionment comparable to the congealing of the moon, the inner freezing' (Gay 1988, p. 525).

There are inevitable losses associated with ageing. There can be a loss of role or status in society, the deaths of peers and the coming into view more sharply of the end of one's own life, as well as the loss of youthful attractiveness and sexual potency. In addition, the threatened or actual experience of what Hess (1987) has described as the 'catastrophes of old age', particularly stroke or dementia, impinge as possibilities even if they do not become realities. They threaten to bring increased dependency on others and loss of the autonomy of younger adulthood, threatening, at least in phantasy if not necessarily in reality, a return to the dependency states of earliest infancy. We also see how for older couples – unable to use work or career and the structure this has afforded them to disperse difficulties, or to contain projections of parts of themselves – an equilibrium they have found earlier on can be upset. As retirement arrives, there is a sense for some couples of being thrown back upon themselves, and of the relationship having to bear or contain things that it had not had to before. Couples can experience this as a demand for increased intimacy and contact with aspects of themselves (possibly experienced as residing in their partner) that have been avoided earlier on. The return to 'twosomeness', and the loss of a wider circle of professional activities and colleagues, can bring a return of claustrophobic anxieties associated with the most intimate relations between mother and infant, of early babyhood and childhood. I shall return to this theme shortly in the clinical material that follows. But lest this sounds too negative, emphasising only what is lost in ageing, 'Getting Older', by Elaine Feinstein (2001, p. 53), strikes a different note:

> The first surprise: I like it.
> Whatever happens now, some things
> that used to terrify have not:
>
> I didn't die young, for instance. Or lose
> my only love. My three children
> never had to run away from anyone.
>
> Don't tell me this gratitude is complacent.
> We all approach the edge of the same blackness
> which for me is silent.
>
> Knowing as much sharpens
> my delight in January freesia,
> hot coffee, winter sunlight. So we say
>
> as we lie close on some gentle occasion:
> every day won from such
> darkness is a celebration.

What is likely to influence whether ageing brings 'sharpened delight', as Feinstein puts it? What factors help to allow a creative engagement with the developmental challenges of old age that will affect whether experience continues to be engaged with in a lively way (which links to the capacity to sustain intimacy later in life)? Freud's early view was that less sexual expression, a decline in genital sexuality, left a problem of undischarged libido, leading to anxiety and other difficulties in old age. Freud (1895, p. 102) wrote about 'the anxiety in senescent men at the time of their decreasing potency and increasing libido', referring to his view that libidinal energy could no longer be discharged via genital sexual activity in the same way anymore, and that this would lead to anxiety and other psychological problems. This was developed by Deutsch (1984), focusing on female sexuality, and the menopause in particular. Like Freud, she believed that in later life the libidinal motor of development essentially goes into reverse gear, bringing psychological problems consequent upon a pathogenic damming up of libido, leading to regression. Deutsch, for example, saw depression as an inevitable feature of the menopause (Bemesderfer 1996). However, subsequent psychoanalytic thinkers have instead taken the view that the impact of such changes will depend upon the individual's capacity to bear loss and the extent to which losses are experienced predominantly in depressive or paranoid schizoid states of mind. This, it is argued, will determine the extent to which experience can continue to be engaged with creatively and intimacy, including sexual intimacy, can be sustained. This links the capacity to adjust to inevitable age-related changes in sexual functioning and the ability to bear the grief that time, in Hardy's words, 'part steals, lets part abide'. The ageing process, with its physical signs such as changes in sexual functioning, taxes the defences that may have been used throughout a lifetime to protect against the spectres of vulnerability, need and dependency awakened by the experience and prospect of loss.

A common loss for men, for example, can be erectile dysfunction. King (1980) points out the importance of the fear of impotence and the impact this may have on relationships in later life. In a review commissioned by the Pennell Initiative for Women's Health and carried out by the Tavistock Centre for Couple Relationships (Vincent et al. 2001) it was pointed out that Havelock Ellis's view in the early twentieth century regarded the menopause as a cut-off point in the sexual life of women, and that in many ways society's attitudes to sexuality in later life have moved on very little since this time. In fact, a number of large-scale research studies have been carried out in recent years showing that although sex may decrease in frequency in old age, older people remain sexually active. These studies highlight how many people adapt to changes in physical health and functioning, sustaining a sexual intimacy that may be expressed in different ways. So an over-emphasis on genital sexuality would give a distorted view of sexuality in old age. The importance of the capacity to adapt and adjust to the changes and losses of old age and to sustain intimacy is highlighted in research that shows that marital closeness moderates the negative psychological impact of functional disability in later life in terms of depression, anxiety and self-esteem (Mancini and Bonanno 2006).

The passage of time, which presages mortality, is a profound loss to be borne. To paraphrase Hardy, 'time makes us grieve'. Freud's view was that we cannot really conceive of our own death, that in the unconscious there is no reference to time, and at an unconscious level we all believe we are immortal – even as we try to imagine our death we are there as observers of our own funeral. However, Money-Kyrle (1971) suggests how, while we might not be able to imagine an abstraction such as death or non-existence, we may nevertheless inherit a 'pre-conception' of it, to use Bion's (1962) term, and we can therefore recognise instances of it. He shows how temporality, the fact of things not lasting, which is a fundamental dimension of all of our experience from the beginning of life, faces us with the threat of the death of our objects and ourselves, and is for everyone an instance of the experience of mortality. This fact of life, that nothing good (or bad) lasts forever, is difficult to accept. It is the capacity to face depressive anxieties that influences our ability to tolerate this, and ultimately affects whether reality is retreated from, with consequent damage to our capacity to engage in a truthful way with our own experience and to sustain intimate relationships with others. Clinically, we can see individuals for whom the mental pain of loss and vulnerability associated with facing the passage of time, and ultimately death, seems impossible to bear. There can be a retreat into rigid and paranoid states of mind, which in couple relationships can present as two partners living in a world peopled by their own projections into one another, resulting in polarised and rigid ways of relating. I shall illustrate what I mean by this in the following clinical example.

The 'No-Change Couple'

He was a successful lawyer, the senior partner in a commercial law firm. She had been an architect. Things had been bad since her retirement two years previously. He was still working, running his firm. They had bought a retirement house and came up to London during the week, staying in their flat while he worked and she tried to occupy herself with charity work and trips to galleries and theatres. Their retirement plans had stalled: he had kept working despite promises to the contrary, and they had never properly moved into the beautiful retirement home in the country that they visited at weekends. What they vividly conveyed to my co-therapist and me when we first met them was how they could not move into and inhabit together the territory of their old age.

At Tavistock Relationships at that time we sent self-report forms to each partner before their first appointment. When this couple came, they told my co-therapist and me that neither of them had read the other's forms, which were sitting, out of sight, side by side on our desk, 'in parallel', so to speak. These forms, each one unknown to the other, sitting like this on the desk, seemed to reflect the parallel lives that the couple lived. This was echoed in the way they each took it in turns to address us in the session, having no direct contact or exchanges with one another. On their forms, each had complained that the other was depressed; she, in particular, had emphasised her worry about his depression.

We had expected, therefore, to meet up with a withdrawn man. In fact, he presented initially as a rather chipper, quite commanding figure, and we were struck instead by her considerable grief and sadness. She was tearful and aggrieved, and it was our feeling, much to our surprise, that she was the depressed one – left waiting for him and frustrated by his unavailability. We thought that feelings of grievance and depression had been lodged in her, and this had been partly provoked by his behaviour and withdrawal into the world of work. He seemed to be keeping a distance both from her and from the depressed part of himself in her through projective identification, such that she was carrying a 'double dose' of depression – his feelings as well as her own. What was striking, as we worked with them over time, was how this depression could move between them, with first she and then he appearing to be the depressed one.

At this early point in our work with them we wondered about the timing of their seeking help, and in relation to this we wondered about the role of retirement as a trigger. It seemed to us that retirement might have threatened a defence that they had previously maintained between them – their parallel lives – where work could function to provide for their need for distance from each other. It was as if, in retirement, they feared being left only with one another, as though their relationship now had to contain all those aspects of themselves that they feared being overwhelmed by and which they had previously managed by taking care that they were never both at risk of being depressed when they might 'both go under at the same time', as they later said.

It was against this background that he presented their dilemma to us: that he felt empty of feeling for his wife. He cared for her, but his feelings of love had vanished. He could not force them to come back, and now he felt tortured. He was, he said, on the brink of separating from her and yet, for some reason, was unable to do so. She seemed to be in an equally tortured position, endlessly waiting for him to make up his mind and to commit to her. The situation was bleak and, as they put it, 'the past is grim, the present is grim and the future is grim'. We referred to this active process of keeping things stuck and unmoving as the act of 'grimming' their experience. The therapy often had a timeless quality, with no sense of urgency or need to sort things out. Though there might be a bit of liveliness or a hint of movement in one session, this would be lost by the next, and we were constantly faced with the complaint that things were just the same, they were stuck in the same old groove. They couldn't separate and they couldn't come together. Feelings seemed to be emptied out, particularly spontaneous feelings, and especially any expression of aggression.

Interestingly, things were a little different when one of them was unable to come to a session and the other came alone. At such times each of them would comment on how much freer they felt than when they were together, that they could say things that they couldn't say when the other one was present for fear that they would be devastated if they were to hear it. While their revelations never felt particularly remarkable, what was striking was their mutual attribution of vulnerability and devastation to the other one. On one such occasion, he commented on what he felt was his difficulty in 'speaking from the heart' to her. I felt there was an echo here in the way he talked of having to be careful with her, of his treatment of my co-therapist and me. For example, we noticed that when he was angry with us he would comment, quite out of the blue, that it was not that he felt furious, not that he felt he was going to explode – when no one had said that he was. This negation was often our first sign that this was precisely what he felt. When we took this up with him he said that he could easily devastate my cotherapist and me. We put it to him that he tended to think of himself always as potentially devastating, never devastated. It then emerged that he had been very upset recently when she had been the one to comment angrily that they should split up. He said that he had been surprised by a comment of his son's, that he thought his mother would manage if they split up, but not his father. This was not how he thought of himself. Then, for the first time, he commented on his uncertainty about himself and what he really felt. It was at this point, when he seemed to glimpse some of his own vulnerability, that his feelings about retirement emerged for the first time. This material led us towards an understanding of their shared underlying fear, or anxiety, that emotional contact could lead to a devastating explosion. It also captured how the fear of a destructive explosion seemed to be closely linked to an underlying fear of loss and separation. It seemed that at some level there was a phantasy operating: that if nothing changed then nothing could be lost.

After a lot of work it emerged very painfully, and with great difficulty, that he had recently had an illness that had left him with sexual difficulties. This was something they found very difficult to speak about. The problems themselves could have been ameliorated by medication, but this would have entailed a reliance upon 'artificial' means to enable sexual intercourse between them, and this was too shameful. His response to his loss of functioning was to feel that he had to work harder than ever. There seemed to be an accusation in his own mind that he was not 'up to it' anymore. He struggled ever more desperately to prove his potency as a manager at work, while avoiding the issue of potency in the sexual relationship. He had withdrawn into an idealisation of self-sufficiency, away from his vulnerability and dependency. He nurtured fantasies of being off on his own. His only imagined future was of himself as a kind of existential anti-hero, on his own in some romantic foreign city. He couldn't envisage a future where they were together. Increasingly, it became evident how unreal these fantasies were. In reality, he could not achieve any separation at all, not even to go away for a holiday, something that she gradually had become able to do. For him, the only separation that was possible was into the world of work, to which he felt equally shackled. Indeed, what we noticed over time was how, when she moved away from her position of being the one who 'wanted' the relationship, and became, in his words, 'more negative', he became 'more positive'. And so they kept themselves in what he termed a zero-sum situation, in which any movement in one direction or another was quickly cancelled out.

How could we understand this situation, where he threatened to leave but where it seemed that no separation at all was possible? Keeping themselves apart in this way seemed to us to be an attempt to obviate any knowledge of the losses that they had already experienced, and that might be facing them. There could be no real discussion of the loss it was clear that at some level he feared if he did retire. This was unthinkable. His response was to work ever more frantically to ablate any knowledge of the reality of his impending retirement. It was very difficult indeed for him to recognise his limitations and the point he had reached in his career, with others expectantly waiting for him to cede his power in the firm to them. He was being asked to give up his potency in his managerial role at work at the same time that he felt he was losing it on so many other fronts.

In our work with this couple, who had for many years been such high achievers, we had a painful sense of the difficulty for them in giving up a lifetime of striving, and moving together into retirement, of realising that the baton, so to speak, is to be passed on now to the next generation. Of course, generational differences and their recognition are central to the story of Oedipus, and this leads us to the question of whether there are particular qualities of the Oedipal situation as it is encountered in later life.

Oedipus and Ageing

The New York Times (25 November 2007) ran a piece describing an increasingly familiar scenario: a former Supreme Court judge found that her husband, who had Alzheimer's disease, was having a relationship with another woman. The judge was reportedly thrilled, 'and even visits the new couple while they hold hands on the porch swing, because it is a relief to see her husband of 55 years so content'. The story explores what the paper called 'old love', illuminating the relationships that often develop among patients with dementia and how the desire for intimacy persists event when dementia takes so much else away. The film *Away from Her*, based on a short story by the Canadian writer Alice Munro, portrays a man watching his wife slip away from him as she is overtaken by the depredations of Alzheimer's disease, only to have to witness, as she moves into residential care, her romance with a male patient in the nursing home. As he struggles with this he eventually moves to a position of accepting the relationship, and arranges for his wife's new love to return to the nursing home after he sees how devastated she is when he is not there. The meaning of this 'acceptance' is understood in relation to his own affairs earlier in the marriage, to his expiation of guilt and remorse, and the reworking of a familiar dynamic in the marriage with him now having to bear the pain of being the excluded one, the witness to the coupling from which he is left out. Here, of course, we are touching on the Oedipal situation, the lifelong struggle to tolerate exclusion, originally from the parental coupling, to recognise that one is not at the exclusive centre of mother's mind but in a position of 'linked separateness' to the parents and their relationship with one another.

The Oedipus complex is never 'resolved' once and for all – we encounter it at different points in the lifespan. In another case, Mrs Jones, a woman in her late eighties, had lost her husband of many years. He had looked after her at their home for some time following her diagnosis of dementia. What had been striking at the time was how she experienced his death. She became convinced that he was not dead at all but that he was alive and seeing another woman instead of her. The delusion that he was still alive but betraying her with another woman might be seen as reflecting unresolved infantile oedipal struggles, underlying difficulties which re-emerged as Mrs Jones's adult cognitive capacities deserted her.

Our current understanding is that earlier problematic emotional constellations do not 'grow old' in the sense of diminishing or fading away, but persist and become more powerful as dependency increases and adult coping falls away, 'because the unconscious does not participate in the process of growing older' (Grotjahn 1940, p. 97).

Ageing is a powerful site for Oedipal anxieties, with the inversion of the earlier Oedipal configuration: for the young it is the parental couple that is procreative, for the old it is the younger generation; the envied object moves from the parents' intercourse to that of the next generation. Something of the challenge that watching children develop into young adults can present for parents is conveyed by a man in late middle age describing the experience of an attractive young woman calling at the house to see his teenaged son:

> At that moment I realised with envy that this young woman hadn't come to see me, she had come to see my son. That was a bit of a shock. A feeling of loss and nostalgia descended on me. I acknowledged to myself that my own days of sexual exploration were over ... If I do allow myself to compare my body with his, I feel more of a sense of loss. Often, it feels like a loss of energy. I can't play football like he does, I feel worn out a lot of the time. [My wife says] I am a grumpy git, so that may well be my unexpressed anger around all of this.
>
> (*The Guardian*, 16 December 2006)

What is being described here is the experience of one generation's displacement by the next, and the re-working of Oedipal anxieties that accompanies experiences of loss and displacement in later life. Klein (1959) comments that identification with the younger generation can help to mitigate these anxieties in older people, just as for the infant identification with the parents' happiness can help to mitigate the painful Oedipal anxieties that are stirred up by the recognition of the parental sexual relationship that excludes the child. She writes:

> This attitude becomes particularly important when people grow older and the pleasures of youth become less and less available. If gratitude for past satisfactions has not vanished, old people can enjoy whatever is still within their reach. Furthermore, with such an attitude, which gives rise

to serenity, they can identify themselves with young people. For instance, anyone who is looking our for young talents and helps to develop them ... is only able to do so because he can identify with others; in a sense he is repeating his own life, sometimes even achieving vicariously the fulfilment of aims unfulfilled in his own life.

(Klein 1959, p. 250)

The riddle of the Sphinx that Oedipus must solve is the task of recognising generational difference, which so often we can try to escape from or triumph over. Shakespeare gave dramatic representation to the Oedipal issues involved in growing older in *King Lear*. At the opening of the play Lear brings together his three daughters and the Court to hear his announcement of his retirement, 'handing over the baton' to the next generation:

> To shake all cares and business from our age
> Conferring them to younger strengths ...
> (*King Lear* 1.1, lines 39–42)

But there is a catch – this is not a gesture born of the serenity that Klein describes. Before they can inherit a third each of his Kingdom his daughters must make a public declaration of their love for him. However, this is not just any declaration of love; they must tell him that they 'love him all'. He must be reassured that he is at the centre of their world and of their affections, rather like the Oedipal child seeking evidence that he is at the centre of his mother's world, wishing to disavow the Oedipal reality that she has other concerns or interests, and a relationship, ultimately, to his father, that excludes him. Cordelia, Lear's youngest daughter, refuses the pressure to repudiate generational differences:

> Why have my sisters husbands, if they say
> They love you all? ... Sure I shall never marry like my sisters
> To love my father all.
> (*King Lear* 1.1, lines 96–104)

Lear rejects the triangular situation in which his truthful daughter faces him with the reality that she loves him, but she also loves her husband to be. This Oedipal situation cannot be managed by Lear, at this point in his life, and so the tragedy of the play unfolds. A place in a triangular relationship is rejected and hated by Lear, and he takes refuge in the delusional appearance of love, an apparent acceptance of increased dependency and loss of power, but 'giving space for younger generations' in an attempt to triumph over and control it.

The play becomes an increasingly nightmarish world of fathers being plotted against by the next generation who wish to displace them. As Edmund, the illegitimate son of the Duke of Gloucester puts it: 'The younger rises when the old doth fall' (*King Lear* 3.3, line 25). What is ushered in is a version of painful loss and relinquishment from one generation to the next that is coloured by the anxieties of the paranoid schizoid position, devoid of gratitude and serenity. The more benign and mature version of the older generation handing over and identifying with the younger, which Klein describes as another developmental possibility, is absent. Lear takes refuge in a delusional world, with a collapse into narcissistic, paranoid and ultimately psychotic states of mind, following on from the point where the reality of generational difference and boundary cannot be recognised. One could see the fears of older figures in *King Lear* of murderous attacks to be a projection of hatred at their own displacement – at the reversal of the original Oedipal configuration – the older generation now giving way to the young, and having to recognise their youthful potency and face a sense of exclusion from the world that goes on without them at the centre anymore. The universal theme of the play is testimony to how painful and difficult this 'passing on of the baton' can be, and how much can go wrong at this developmental phase.

Such dramas are not, of course, confined to the stage but appear in the consulting rooms of psychotherapists working with couples, as my final clinical example illustrates. There are some similarities with the first couple that I described, and, indeed, I find that couples frequently come for help in later life when they can no longer use sexuality and work as they did in younger days to manage difficulties in sustaining intimacy between them.

When a Couple's Familiar Defences No Longer Hold Up

The couple were just entering later life, and facing depression as life-long defences were wearing thin, he having had affairs throughout the marriage and now confronted by impotence as a consequence of treatment for prostate cancer. Ostensibly, the couple came for help because of his affairs over the course of their forty-year marriage. However, pretty quickly it became clear that it was not the affairs, so much, that were the reason for their seeking help at this point. They had made a lifelong defensive use of sexuality, he through his numerous affairs and she in both tolerating the situation and, at the same time, investigating and seeking to expose them. And the experience of prostate cancer triggered a response in the husband that was the same as at other points in his life when he had had difficulties: he had another affair. It was short-lived, and, though it re-ignited the compelling drama between them (which, in reality, did not seem to need an actual 'other woman' to sustain it), it also exposed their difficulty in facing the loss, vulnerability, and dependency brought into prospect by the beginning of old age, a prospect that for each of them threatened a traumatic return of the dependency of their infancy and childhood where each had, in different ways, lost their opposite-sex parent.

The couple had met when they were both very young, and had come to the UK as adults where they had raised a family. They rarely returned to their country of origin, though spoke, on occasion, about moving back to live in the 'mother country'. Both partners shared earlier experiences of failed dependency. He was a man who had barely seen his mother for the first seven years or so of his life, as she had constantly been ill, hospitalised in isolation wards for fear of infection. She had lost her father at the age of eight, and subsequently the family home had broken-up and the children were sent away to boarding school.

In the marriage, each partner showed a profound difficulty in tolerating their dependency on the other, a fear of dependency that had worsened with age and his experience of a failing body. His prowess, both on the sports field and in his capacity to attract women sexually, were very important to him. Yet with the onset of old age, he had had two hip replacements and prostate cancer in quick succession, the treatment of which had left him with erectile difficulties: 'I am old from the waist down', he explained to me.

His wife was always kept guessing, worried about where he was, fearful of abandonment by him, so reversing his early childhood situation of abandonment by mother. Now, he was the desired object of attention and she the abandoned one, never able to trust in his dependability. Even with the rugby teams he played for he would agree to appear in two or three matches on the same Saturday afternoon, and at the last minute he would let them down, feeling himself to be the indispensable, much-wanted player, with all the teams vying in his mind's eye to have him. When I first saw them he was still going on three-mile runs, trying to prove to himself that he could do the same things as ever, even though he had been told that this was damaging his hips and causing him serious physical problems. Later life had faced him with a very difficult re-adjustment. Defences that he had used throughout his life – his use of sexuality and manic activity – could not be sustained in the same way anymore. Between them, they repeatedly enacted a very familiar situation of accusation and cover up, investigation and exposure. This had a timeless quality, and together they would go around and around this well-trodden ground. The situation in the therapy seemed to be one where each made representations to me, as though I were the judge in a courtroom investigating their respective accusations of the other. More contact with need and dependency quickly got turned into an investigation that would expose one or other of them – he as having been 'caught at it', exposed as a liar and cheat, she as being 'mad' and pathologically jealous. This seemed to be an excited dramatisation of their painful Oedipal struggle. Consciously, they hated it, but at the same time there was a triumph in this state of mind over more painful feelings.

They started to recognise the pattern, and a different picture of him began to emerge from the self-confident 'Casanova' that both of them had encouraged me to see. When this was taken up he would quickly get into a superior, contemptuous position. Indeed, they would join together to position themselves as the couple with all the resources, a triumphant, omnipotent state, where they felt envied by other people of whom they were contemptuous, 'people who drive old cars'. They joked about their contempt for people with Clarks shoes, a symbol of being old and sensible, they said, that they weren't ready for yet – shoes that I was clearly wearing. He commented that he needed to be different from his parents' flat and nothing life. In this omnipotent state of mind he reduced his parents to flat and lifeless figures, in the same way as he denied the existence of the vulnerable aspects of himself by triumphing over his need and dependency on his internal good objects and his therapist.

As time went on he reported feeling more depressed, and she spoke of feeling more trusting of him. It felt to me that he was able to be in a more truthful contact with himself. On one occasion she described how she had tried to touch him affectionately and he hadn't responded. This quickly turned into an argument between them in the room, but the atmosphere shifted, when he became able to talk about his fear that more intimate contact between them might lead to sex. 'I have to get this bloody thing – the pump – out, it's a bloody great thing, not very attractive. It's not like me, not to try things to help myself', he said. But it faced him with what had changed, and with having to depend on something else for help, and to acknowledge his need for it. I thought that this linked to his sense of shame and exposure in recognising his need for the therapy, and for his younger therapist.

He then commented on how he couldn't use the pump at home because his (grown up) children would see it, and spoke of how the onset of his feelings of depression were linked to envy of a younger couple who didn't have to work so hard, and who seemed to have it all. In the transference I thought he was communicating something important about how it felt to be showing me his fears and what was failing him, and his envy of my relative youth. When I took this up, he spoke of his fears that if he did try these aids they might not work, and then he would be left feeling that there was nothing that could help him. What he conveyed was how he no longer had access to defences he used to rely on, and that he feared he'd be left with nothing in their place, exposed by his sense of need and dependency, which I thought were linked to feelings of shame. He imagined using the pump, and it taking half an hour or more to have an effect. He said he could imagine her getting fed up. He was anxiously looking at her while he talked, scrutinising her face for her reaction. And then he spoke movingly about his fears about what she felt about the changes in him. It was very difficult for him to put these into words, but when he did so there was a glimpse of an emotional contact between them, which they found very difficult to sustain. Towards the end of the session, when I took up how they moved away so quickly from the point of contact between them, he commented 'they are losses aren't they, it's like a bereavement really, losing your potency'.

They described going for a walk together, on a beach on holiday. As they got to the beach they had had an explosive row, something that came on very suddenly and violently. She'd gone off in the other direction away from him. The row had been sparked by her trying to look after him, telling him they should get out of the wind, and he had felt controlled by her. It was a poignant image of the possibility of intimacy between them, of being able to look after one another, but in the face of this came an explosive row, each moving off in opposite directions, sitting far apart from the other, on different rocks, looking at the sunset. They conveyed the difficulty in facing the evening of their lives together, in helping each other and allowing an intimacy with one another in which they would have to face their own and the other's ageing and losses – the changes in themselves also reflecting the changes in the other.

In such couples, who have encountered profound difficulties in facing the passage of time, it is as if they find themselves living with images of themselves in their partner that they find increasingly difficult to bear. In this way, the partners in the couple reflected to one another the reality of their ageing, literally represented by the older body now in front of them that contains the truth of time passing, confronting them with all the difficulties of facing this 'fact of life'.

Ageing, Oppression, and Opportunity

I want to conclude this chapter by returning to my starting point, to the poem by Hardy, and his sense of being oppressed by the changes of age, 'wasting skin', the difficulty of still having a full heart and desires and at the same time knowing about the changes and losses of age. It is, as Hardy puts it, the 'part stolen/part abiding' that brings forth grief: the continued life of the body and the mind, the awareness of desires and, at the same time, of physical changes such as the loss of youthful physical attractiveness and potency. A solution can be to wish away the desire, to 'shrink the heart', in Hardy's words – to withdraw from bringing to life sexual desire or involvement and intimacy, which also then brings to life the grief at what is no longer. This was frequently the solution of the couples I have described, reflecting lifelong difficulties with intimacy that were compounded by the developmental pressures of later life, the difficulty in mourning the losses that were facing them.

In his marriage, Hardy had 'frozen' his heart for many years before the death of his first wife (Tomalin 2006a). It was his wife Emma's death at the age of seventy-two that produced an outpouring of poems about her, and established his reputation as a poet. These poems work and re-work his feelings about the marriage, which seems to have become an increasingly estranged one with the passing of the years. In them, one glimpses the pain of his attempts to make reparation to her after she has gone – with the memory of early love and intimacy between them that has become hard and cold in their withdrawal from one another in later life. This poem he entitled *Penance* (in Tomalin 2006b, p. 134):

> 'Why do you sit, O pale thin man
> At the end of the room
> By that harpsichord, built on the quaint old plan?
> – It is as cold as a tomb,
> And there's not a spark within the grate:
> And the jingling wires
> Are as vain desires
> That have lagged too late.'
>
> 'Why do I? Alas, far times ago
> A woman lyred here
> In the evenfall; one who fain did so
> From year to year;
> And, in loneliness bending wistfully,
> Would wake each note
> In sick sad rote,
> None to listen or see!'
>
> 'I would not join, I would not stay,
> But drew away,
> Though the fire beamed brightly ... Aye!
> I do to-day
> What I would not then; and the chill old keys,
> Like a skull's brown teeth
> Loose in their sheath,
> Freeze my touch; yes, freeze.'

Hewison (2006) has pointed out how, in this poem, Hardy conveys the painful recognition of his retreat from the possibility of emotional warmth with his wife, and his guilt for killing her off, in his heart, many years before her actual death. What strikes me is how Hardy describes his own 'inner freezing', as Freud put it, recognising the part of himself that withdrew from the life between them, and which now becomes linked to the chill thought both of her life that is gone and his own death to come. As the reader, this puts us in vivid contact with the difficulty of facing what we have done with the possibility of intimacy and life in our relationships, a struggle that we all have throughout our lives, and one that is given a particular quality and intensity in old age when faced with finality and the limits of reparation, of the years having passed, and with actual death. How difficult it can be to allow insight, to take responsibility for our own destructiveness, and to face depressive anxieties when the scope for actual repair may be gone: when these difficulties, which we all encounter at significant points of change or loss in our lives, cannot any more be dealt with by projecting into the future the thoughts of what we will do differently, reassuring us of our potential for reparation. While this may make for great difficulty and challenge in later life, born of the fear that now it is 'too late', it can also be the case that an awareness of the limits of time passing, and of time remaining, can bring an urgency and motivation to the wish to work through past losses and to face future ones.

Hardy's poems, written late in his life, bring home with great poignancy how, although the opportunity for real repair of his relationship with his wife had passed, the work of internal reparation was given its greatest urgency, and he is brought into sharper contact than before with his inner situation, and with his need to face this – his reparative wishes bringing the flowering of a creative lyrical outpouring in his last years. Needless to say, sexuality, with all of its vicissitudes and significance in relational terms, continues for us throughout life, with familiar age-old conflicts as well as the demands of adjusting to changes in functioning and tolerating the waning of capacities. These painful realities, particularly Oedipal ones, as I have tried to show, have new coinages in old age, yet they reflect what at heart we struggle with all of our lives.

References

Bemesderfer, S. (1996). A Revised Psychoanalytic View of Menopause. *Journal of the American Psychoanalytic Association*, 44S, 351–369.

Bion, W. R. (1962). A Theory of Thinking. *International Journal of Psycho-Analysis*, 38, 266–275.

Deutsch, H. (1984). The Menopause. *International Journal of Psycho-Analysis*, 65, 55–62.

Feinstein, E. (2001). Getting Older. In W. Cope (ed.), *Heaven on Earth: 101 Happy Poems*. Faber & Faber.

Freud, S. (1895). On the Grounds for Detaching a Particular Syndrome from Neurasthenia under the Description 'Anxiety Neurosis'. In J. Strachey (ed. and trans.), *The Standard Edition of the Works of Sigmund Freud, Vol. 3*. Hogarth Press.

Freud, E., Freud, L. and Grubrich-Simitis, I. (1978). *Sigmund Freud: His Life in Pictures and Words*. Penguin.

Gay, P. (1988). *Freud: A Life for Our Time*. Pan Macmillan.

Grotjahn, M. (1940). Psychoanalytic Investigation of a Seventy-One Year Old Man with Senile Dementia. *Psychoanalytic Quarterly*, 9, 80–97.

Hess, N. (1987). King Lear and Some Anxieties of Old Age. *British Journal of Medical Psychology*, 60, 209–215.

Hewison, D. (2006). *Thoughts on Creativity and the Internal Couple*. Presented at Freud 150th Anniversary Seminars, Maudsley Hospital Psychotherapy Unit, 7 December.

King, P. (1980). The Life Cycle as Indicated by the Nature of the Transference in the Psychoanalysis of the Middle-Aged and Elderly. *International Journal of Psycho-Analysis*, 61, 153–160.

Klein, M. (1959). Our Adult World and its Roots in Infancy. In M. Klein, *Envy and Gratitude and Other Works 1946–1963*. Hogarth Press.

Mancini, A. and Bonanno, G. (2006). Marital Closeness, Functional Disability and Adjustment in Late Life. *Psychology and Aging*, 21(3), 600–610.

Money-Kyrle, R. (1971). The Aim of Psychoanalysis. *International Journal of Psycho-Analysis*, 52, 103–106.

Stearns, P. (1979). The Evolution of Traditional Culture Toward Aging. In J. Hendricks and C. Davis (Eds.) *Dimensions in Ageing: Readings*. Winthorp Publishers.

Tomalin, C. (2006a). *Thomas Hardy: The Time Torn Man*. Penguin.

Tomalin, C. (2006b). *Poems of Thomas Hardy*. Penguin.

Vincent, C., Riddell, J. and Shmueli, A. (2001). *Sexuality and Older Women: Setting the Scene*. Pennell Paper No. 1. Pennell Initiative for Women's Health.

Chapter 3

Another Country?
Migration, Displacement, and Internal Dislocation in Old Age

'I find myself remembering an advertising slogan which said: why live, when you can be buried for $10?'

Freud wrote this in a letter to Marie Bonaparte in the last year of his life, after he had arrived as a refugee in England. Dislocation is part of the personal history of psychoanalysis – diaspora the experience of many of the first generation of analysts. In this chapter, I am going to think about the internal experience of dislocation consequent upon ageing itself – where psychically, if not geographically, one might find oneself in a foreign land. Rack (1982) describes dislocation occurring when the psychological cues that help an individual to function in society are withdrawn and replaced with new ones. Perhaps this highlights the common elements facing the migrant moving from one country to another, and the dis-location experienced in the crossing over, into old age, of those who stay at home – both may be faced with a new psychological, as well as social, context.

The poet Elaine Feinstein (2007), writing of her husband's death, put it like this in her poem 'Afghan':

> My taxi driver yesterday was an Afghan
> Living in London for some years.
> What he misses most, he explained, was
> the sense that what he does matters to anyone.
> There are no gains.
>
> His neighbours rarely provoke him to more than
> flickers of shame or occasional adrenalin.
> He is in exile. Tonight I am alone,
> Simply a woman sitting undressed in
> an Edward Hopper bedroom.

The Social Context of Displacement in Old Age

At a social level, our notion of history as the story of the linear march of progress can carry with it the attribution that earlier generations were somehow not fully human like us – not so evolved. Think of the construction of 'the Dark Ages' (which recently has been reinterpreted as a time when a great many very enlightened and creative developments were achieved). This is perhaps a version of history that is a product of a youth culture. Socially, if not personally, things are always improving. In this is a denial of an identification with previous generations. T. S. Eliot:

> It seems, as one becomes older,
> That the past has another pattern, and ceases to be a mere sequence –
> Or even development: the latter a partial fallacy
> Encouraged by superficial notions of evolution,
> Which becomes, in the popular mind, a means of disowning
> the past.
>
> (Eliot 1944, p. 26)

Literature or art of the past can put us in touch with the humanity of previous generations, how they were struggling with the same human dilemmas. And when we allow ourselves to know this, to see beyond the differences of language, dress, technology, then we see that we are like them and that we will die as they have died. It is difficult for us to know about old age and the end of life, so we tend to keep it out of view, another country, where we have difficulty imagining ourselves dwelling.

Seeking temporarily to enter this world, the journalist Zoe Williams donned a prosthetic face to make herself look like an older woman.

> I realised that I was invisible in the sense that people literally could not see me ... At the top of the escalator... a woman backs me into a shoulder-high plant pot ... she walks backwards into me, and carries on walking until I have my elbow pressed into pebbly earth ... I say, 'What an earth do you think you're doing?' And she just flicks her eyes at me and moves on; she doesn't even do me the courtesy of returning my rage.
>
> (*The Guardian*, 28 October 2006)

Old age is excluded from ordinary currency, and many everyday phrases convey this: the 'digital divide', the 'generation gap'. A newspaper editorial put it like this:

> The average Briton dies in semi-darkness, is cremated behind drawn curtains, and has no public memorial. The shared presence of death that was common in other times or societies has been lost in ours.
>
> (*The Guardian*, 17 February 2009)

And, in getting rid of death, we also have to dispose of old age. Social research conveys in quantitative terms the human cost of this. The UK Inquiry into Mental Health and Wellbeing in Later Life estimated that one million older people in the UK are socially isolated and projected this to rise to 2.2 million over the next fifteen years if it is not addressed (Lee 2006).

But we are not only concerned here with 'external' or socially driven experiences of displacement. There can be an internal difficulty too – of being displaced from a sense of oneself – on crossing into the territory of old age. 'Old age is particularly difficult to assume because we have always regarded it as something alien, a foreign species: "can I have become a different being while I still remain myself?"' (de Beauvoir 1972, p. 315). As we move past the mid-point in our lives, we cross what the writer Joseph Conrad called the 'shadow line' of our generation – where we move over the brow of the hill to view, on the other side, the prospect of our mortality (see Segal 1984). Jacques (1965) describes a crisis at mid-life, stimulated by the awareness of encroaching mortality, which must be worked through in order for creativity to be sustained. Are there other 'shadow lines' that are crossed in later life, associated with displacement: both external, from the social world where old age is poor currency, and also internally, in our sense of ourselves, as Simone de Beauvoir suggests?

Perhaps one answer is in the displacement in time that we may experience as our lives unfold – as the world we knew changes, and yet stays the same. According to Jacques's formulation, I am well into, or indeed well beyond, the point of crisis. And I am sometimes disconcerted as my childhood, and the world of the sixties and seventies, is referred to now by my own children as 'the olden days'. As they get older – and this is what many older people coming into services convey – it is as if the world that they know has left them behind – and they find themselves living as foreigners – refugees in time – exiled from the familiar – and living in a world where they feel they have lost their place. The journalist Katherine Whitehorn (2007), writing about the experience of bereavement in later life: 'You don't get over the man, though you do, after a year or two, get over the death; but you have to learn to live in another country in which you are an unwilling refugee…'

'Displacements In and Out of Time'

The novelist Penelope Lively said in an interview:

> In old age, you realise that while you're divided from your youth by decades, you can close your eyes and summon it at will … The idea that memory is linear is nonsense … As to time itself – can it be linear when all these snatches of other presents exist at once in your mind?
>
> (*The Guardian*, 25 July 2009)

Baroness Warnock said:

> A bar or two of Sibelius's fourth symphony and I am back in 1948, with everything ahead ... I can never quite believe people who say – even though I am 80, I feel just the same as I always did ... How can they feel the same when their body, including their brain which is what they actually are, is running down?
>
> (*The Observer*, 17 May 2009)

As I wrote this, I could see Telecom Tower, with its revolving neon sign counting down the days to the 2012 Olympics above me, an inescapable charting of the passage of days going by. Psychoanalytically, two essential dimensions of time are distinguished: the atemporal unconscious mind, of primary process, the moveable nature of the psychic experience of time, regression and *après-coup*, for example; and linear, diachronic time – the reality of where one is in one's lifetime. Two seams, the atemporal unconscious world in which the contents of a lifetime sit together, undiminished and unseparated by the passage of time, on the one hand, and on the other, the reality of temporality and limits of time passing: these are the potentially conflicting dimensions of time in our psychic life. They are brought into sharp focus as we 'get towards the end of the line', so to speak. How the crossing of the 'shadow line' in later life, and awareness of mortality, is experienced depends on the relationship to diachronic time – on the capacity to tolerate the losses that the passing of time brings.

Conrad's 'shadow line' is an interesting image: a line is a liminal point – implying a crossing from one state to another. Indeed, the idea of a mid-life crisis has within it the notion of a critical point, which requires a working through at a particular developmental stage in the lifespan. However, while a shadow has an outline, it is also diffuse – it casts itself across a space – in this case, across a lifespan – as children develop an idea of, and a primitive understanding of, death; but its contours become sharper as one gets closer to it. The consequences of this knowledge of death are profound – perhaps giving shape to one's life – providing a point of perspective and definition of 'the road travelled', as the psychoanalyst Quinodoz (2009) puts it, but anxieties associated with death and defensive responses to this knowledge can also be profoundly disabling:

> There are times when, on the journey through life – especially as it draws to a close – people forget that they are travelling ... all that remains is the monotony of everyday existence ... However ... the very savour of life is linked to the fact that it is by nature transient ... by unconsciously effacing death, so too the interesting features of life are lost – 'because the prospect of its end, gives shape to the journey'.
>
> (Quinodoz 2009, p. 31)

This latter point is very close to the view of the philosopher Heidegger (1929) – that the meaning of existence is in the fact of our death – he writes of 'existence towards death' (*Dasein zum Tode*), and he sees this as fundamental to our apprehension of time. Money-Kyrle (1971) also describes as one of the 'facts of life' our experience of transience, in the everyday losses of life, that signal the loss of our objects and, ultimately, ourselves. The transition to old age, and the losses this augurs, can be associated with a psychic retreat from engagement with life and experience – as though to 'freeze time'. I shall explain what I mean by this shortly.

Freud (1915, p. 296) disagrees with the view that death provides a point of perspective, from which reflection on our selves springs, saying that, in taking this position, 'the philosophers are being too philosophical'. Instead of a view of rational humanity, contemplating its own end, Freud's notion is that 'Our unconscious does not believe in its own death; it behaves as if it were immortal.' Freud distinguishes between the fear of death and the death instinct; fear of death is linked to Eros, to the life instinct – and the tumult of life is the operation of the libidinal instincts, which are protective against the death instinct.

This is perhaps captured in the famous poem by Dylan Thomas (1952), writing about the death of his father – 'Do not go gentle into that good night':

> Wild men who caught and sang the sun in flight,
> And learn, too late, they grieved it on its way,
> Do not go gentle into that good night.
> Grave men, near death, who see with blinding sight
> Blind eyes could blaze like meteors and be gay,
> Rage, rage against the dying of the light.

In a discussion of the fear of death, Freud speculates:

> It would be possible to picture the id as under the domination of the mute but powerful death instincts, which desire to be at peace and (prompted by the pleasure principle) to put Eros, the mischief-maker, to rest.
>
> (Freud 1923, p. 59)

This links the discussion of the fear of death to a different situation, not where the fight for life in the face of death is central (which links to the conflict between life and death – the wish for life) but a situation where the id is, instead, under the domination of the death instinct. Birksted-Breen (2009) describes the situation that she observes clinically, of a withdrawal into an atemporal state connected to the wish for Nirvana (an expression of the death instinct according to Freud) which she links to the inability to mourn and hence to symbolise, leading to a 'freezing of time'. This idea may help us to understand the clinical phenomenon, whereby instead of conflict and anxiety in relation to knowledge of death or the passing of time – the struggle to sustain life – there appears instead to be a retreat into a more deadly state, where an equilibrium is maintained at the cost of stasis and a retreat from reality, the passage of time, and the losses that our transience brings. The difficulty with such a retreat is that the Nirvana principle is not just regressive to an early pleasure principle, but is also destructive of good objects – leaving the person without resources for life or for facing death, as Brearley (2005) points out.

The Buddhist legend of the early life of Prince Siddhartha describes how his father, in an effort to defy the prophecy that his son would renounce the family and follow a spiritual destiny, tried to prevent him from seeing the signs of ageing, sickness and death. When, despite his father's efforts, one day he ventures forth and encounters these realities of life, he responds:

> 'If all must face old age, then how can we take joy in youth?
> 'If all must face death, then how can we delight in life?'
> The prince returns to the palace – and announces – 'no more do I care for parks or pleasure, or anything that may pass away. Soon I too will renounce this life that binds me ...'
>
> (Shepard 1995, p. 45)

This conveys the attempt to maintain a retreat from the realities of loss, ageing, and mortality, a retreat that ultimately can't be sustained, and how difficult it is to face these realities, and to value 'anything that may pass away'. 'Psychic retreats' or 'pathological organisations' are described by a number of writers, such as Rosenfeld (1964), O'Shaughnessy (1981), and Steiner (1987, 1993). They describe a particular fixed structure of defences in which the aim is to maintain a psychic equilibrium (Reisenberg-Malcolm 1988 [1970]) outside the normal fluctuation between the paranoid-schizoid and depressive positions. Steiner describes, in addition, a perverse aspect, the gratification derived from the self-sufficiency of this state, which offers 'the comforts of withdrawal to a state which is neither fully alive nor quite dead ... and relatively free of pain and anxiety' (Steiner 1993, p. 24). These organisations are seen as always pathological, interfering with development, and, although they may allow for a restricted type of life, they have to be given up for a true contact with reality to be achieved. As the 'retreat' functions as an enclave, away from the anxieties of the paranoid-schizoid and depressive positions, emergence from it threatens to expose the individual to such anxieties, so that movement out of the retreat might be felt as a psychic disaster. In this state of psychic retreat, there is no transience – if we are in touch with the possibility of transitions, we know that nothing lasts forever (and, as Money-Kyrle 1971 points out, this is an instance of the experience of finitude, of the death of our objects and ourselves).

As Bell (2006) says, the feeling of oneself existing in time is an important developmental achievement, but for some is a catastrophe to be avoided by retreat into a timeless world. The pull into these states can affect us at any age. But perhaps we can see a particular form of this in some older people, associated with a psychic stasis, a retreat into a more timeless state where, as Quinodoz (2009) observes, losses, and ultimately death, are effaced. As Bronstein (2002) points out, the wish for immortality may not simply be a desire to live forever, but at a deeper level arise from the difficulty of facing vulnerability and loss, death being the ultimate expression of such vulnerability. In the transition to old age, the work of mourning becomes more urgent. But the limits of time left for reparation can also, perhaps, make it difficult for depressive anxieties to be faced, when there may be the feeling that there is not enough time left to repair things. I shall now turn to clinical examples of people presenting for psychological help for the first time in later life and will be conceptualising these cases in terms of psychic retreat in later life.

A woman in her late seventies presented with feelings of depression, which seemed to have been precipitated by retirement from her academic position, as a consequence of health difficulties. Her husband had died several years earlier and her grown-up children lived abroad. From her point of view, she had managed these experiences well, and the current depression was not felt to be linked to anything in particular for her. She seemed to inhabit an ethereal, untouchable state, and the sessions were characterised by a daydreamy quality. She spoke of how she loved walking alone on the beach – such a peaceful state of mind, she got very absorbed in that, she said. She tried to withdraw into a meditative state, where she let her thoughts pass by, undisturbed – 'like still water'. Though she also worried that she lacked the capacity for connection with other people, and in the sessions, the absorption into a daydream state interfered with her wish to get help. I felt that I could drift into a way of thinking with her that felt stereotypic – my interpretations could feel 'samey' and lifeless, or alternatively as an unwelcome intrusion on a state of mind whereby she tried to keep herself undisturbed and out of contact with difficult feelings.

Over time, there were increasing moments of contact, but these seemed to be quickly followed by retreat. She presented her withdrawal as stepping back to breathe and review things, but this was not the quality of it. It seemed instead that something more active was happening – a 'killing off' of contact, and then she felt hit by persecutory anxiety for 'messing it up'. As she felt herself to be more involved, she was exposed to the pain of the reality of her ageing and her vulnerability – she became more in touch with her physical frailty and her anxieties about dying alone – but this, in turn, seemed to lead to an intensification of her defences: she spoke of feeling more involved in life, but at the same time, of a need to withdraw 'into a feeling of stillness, silence ... like there's always a pressure to go back to that', to escape from the depressive anxieties into the area of her retreat, which seemed to provide, as Steiner (1987) describes, an illusion of stability and a relative freedom from anxiety and pain.

As the therapy went on, there came a point when it seemed that she was becoming less able to sustain her retreat, and there was some loosening of its grip, including the illusion of timelessness. She became preoccupied about a deadline for a piece of work she had been asked to produce, and which she had ignored while being contemptuous of a colleague who was trying to remind her of the time limit she faced. Around this time, she also became extremely anxious about the possibility of a leak in her flat and desperately tried to keep various areas sealed, while feeling it was impossible to make her flat waterproof. We explored this in relation to the increasing sense of panic that she could no longer 'seal' her mind from an awareness of time. It seemed that part of her was now more able to know about time limits, which couldn't be kept out. This allowed more contact with her anxieties about the real deadline she was facing, her panic about ageing and death.

There was a painful atmosphere in the months following where at times she seemed more in touch with the realities of her life, but alongside this, restoring her previous equilibrium, her gloomy state. 'I have noticed how I can't cope with things feeling important for long, without needing a sort of rest. I have to retrace my footsteps and go back to the gloomy feeling for a while ...'

She then described how it reminded her of the time in her childhood when her father had died. She had gone, as a girl, for long walks on her own and felt this same sense of 'gloom'. The adults, especially her mother, were, she said, all in a grim way, and she described how she used to hide herself away in bushes at the end of the garden, where nobody could find her. There was a painful atmosphere in the session. Then, there was a shift in this, and her next comment suggested how the retreat became idealised:

> It sounds as though I am romanticising it ... I really like gloomy weather because that's what I remember at the time, sort of sitting in the garden and watching the rain. It was gloomy, but at the same time, it felt like a relief ... I think I do that now when I go for my long walks.

It felt to me, at that moment, that she had 'walked away', so to speak, in the session, from a painful moment of contact, returning to the safety of her retreat. She conveyed a picture of a child for whom none of the adults could provide the containment she needed, leaving her to cope with the loss of her father on her own, witnessing her mother collapsing. It seemed that she continued to feel left on her own throughout her life, without a proper foundation for dealing with loss.

At one session in this period, she told me how she could try to keep out of sight, withdraw, and sit in the dark, as if making herself dead, unable to be bothered to do anything, to switch the light on, and this state of withdrawal continued, at times, to be evident in her sessions. She spoke of how it felt like she suddenly 'came to' after a period like this and felt very panicky and anxious, 'that I have to make up for lost time'. I thought that she could feel a sense of panic after a session, when she felt she had killed things off and came back, anxious to make up for lost time, and worried about how much time she had lost. At the end of this session, she described starting to remember how she felt about things in the past, 'feelings I haven't remembered for a long time', and she described how she had taken out of a box of old recordings of herself playing the piano that she used to make as a younger woman, music that she had played for the first time in years.

In one way, she could want to keep out of sight, not want me to see, her hatred and capacity to kill things off, part of herself that she constantly tried to dismiss or disown and was frightened might overwhelm her. It seemed that her obsessionality was a defence against this killing off of feelings, of her object, which threatened to leave her completely disconnected. The state of being cut off in that way may in one way have been a relief, the retreat into a state where she did not have to feel, where everything became meaningless. It seemed that I was felt to be cutting her off from this retreat and that she constantly needed to check that the 'gloomy' state of mind, as she put it, was still available. However, I also felt that she was allowing more contact with me, trying to 'take things out of the box', to let me listen more to how her mind worked. It seemed that, at this point, she felt safe enough to start to show me more of her deeper anxieties.

The ending came as a consequence of my leaving my post, and there were several months during which the ending was known about and anticipated. She oscillated, in the period coming up to the ending, between pulling back into the retreat and moments when she was more in contact. She spoke a number of times, about how it was part of her culture, her religion, to believe that in the latter part of life, you should withdraw from people, detach yourself, otherwise your spirit could become trapped. But then, she could allow me to see something much more in touch and anguished:

> I can get so preoccupied with all that's negative, sort of see nothing else, only bad things and then I get overwhelmed by feelings of giving up, feeling there's no point. It's like the accusing thoughts in my head, saying there's mess everywhere and nothing can be done, there's no time and I feel I have to cancel things or give up.

I took up how she felt that I was leaving her in a mess, without time to sort things out, that she felt I was giving up on her with the ending. She then made a comment in a very clear and emphatic tone of voice. She said that therapy had cleared a path in her mind and she was frightened that it would get completely swamped with things, and she could easily feel she had no connections. I commented on the pull back into a state of mind where she's disconnected, as well as her fear of it. She said, 'Yes, the sessions have always given me a way back in.' It seemed that she was aware that she needed her sessions, this was not yet an internalised capacity, and that consequently the ending was felt to be terrifying for her. It felt to me that she conveyed her experience that the therapy was moving away from her, but at the same time, her retreat was not available to her in the same way anymore, and she feared being left falling between the two.

At the final session, she spoke of how she had always felt that she could come back and mend things, and that helped. 'But now, that's it and I can't come back.' In her words, there was 'not enough time to mend things'. She needed to cover everything that might come into her mind later, to do with having said something critical or attacked me, or simply not used the sessions well. I felt she was conveying her fear of being left in a hostile state of mind, stirred up by the ending, faced with depressive anxieties with the sense that there was not enough time to work them through. She had perhaps been brought into therapy as the defences she had relied upon started to break down in her later years – as she was faced with the threat of dependency and ill health. In this sense, she was entering new territory, as her defences no longer functioned for her in the same way anymore, and her movements out of her retreat faced her with anxieties that had been fended off. In this sense, she was facing 'new and foreign territory' at the same time as the return of familiar anxieties and difficulties. Martindale (1989) points out how the threat of dependency as people get older – and the breakdown of defences that may have sustained them in younger adulthood – can bring a 'return' of earlier trauma and difficulty, particularly for people such as my patient, for whom dependency in childhood was associated with failures of containment, and loss and breakdown in their objects. The return of the spectre of dependency is then associated with trauma and breakdown – a breakdown that has already happened.

I felt a painful sense of leaving her before she was ready, of her fragile point of development that might not be sustained. And of the difficulty for her in emerging, at this point in her life, to face losses, and the knowledge of the internal restrictions that had limited her relationships in her younger years. With this patient, I had both the sense of the profound difficulty in moving out of the psychic retreat, which put her in contact with painful realities and anxieties, and yet of the development that was also possible, however fragile I felt it to be.

It is an interesting question, how much what may look like a 'psychic retreat' may also resemble descriptions in the literature that are offered as something much more developmental, and specific to later life. The sociologist Thornstam (1997, p. 150) puts forward the notion of 'gerotranscendence', a shift from the competitive values of younger adulthood to a wider view of reality. In interviews with older adults, respondents said things like: 'My best times now are when I sit on the kitchen porch and simply exist, the swallows flying about my head like arrows.' This may be similar to what Quinodoz (2009) describes as the 'Blue Note' – a moment of connection with a feeling of transcendence, in which there is a sense of engagement with something vital, both within and beyond the self. This has a different quality from the internal situation of my patient, where the encroaching realities of ageing seemed to be linked to a state of retreat, in which her good objects, and what was of value to her internally, were destroyed, leaving her in an impoverished state, and setting up a profound persecutory guilt which compounded the problem, fuelling the need to retreat.

I felt guilty for leaving her at this point – for what hadn't been achieved in the therapy – which was also, for her, linked to the life that had not been possible – the need to mourn the life that had not been lived. In my countertransference, this was compounded because the ending was consequent upon my moving on – my own development and the different point in the lifespan that I was at. Mourning what could not now be achieved or realised was an important aspect of the ending and can be an important theme in working with older people. However, what cannot in reality be changed does not obviate the need for internal reparation – the need to 'put some order inside with respect to objects that were important – to improve the internal relationships – to keep them alive internally', as Quinodoz (2009) puts it.

For all of us, the losses that are current in our lives will reawaken, at an unconscious level at least, earlier experiences of loss. Where there is not the internal support for facing losses and the diminution of capacities in later life, then defences may have to be increased, and for some people, may no longer hold up at the point when they are most needed, leading them into the internal refuge of psychic retreat. I am discussing here a particular cohort of people, who, although they may have had profound early losses and difficulties, seem to have coped in younger adulthood, only presenting for help for the first time in later life. Often, I have noticed this occurring when certain kinds of use have been made of work or sexuality – or just a constant 'moving on' earlier on – to avoid facing loss and limitations, guilt, and the need for reparation. I have seen a number of people presenting for help when this cannot any longer be sustained. Loss of capacity, retirement, insults to physical health – all of these typical features of old age confront the individual with difficulties and limitations that can no longer be 'outrun' in the same way anymore. I think some of these themes are evident in the following case example.

Working with a Couple – the Displacement of Entering Old Age

> When marrying, ask yourself this question: do you believe that you will be able to converse well with this person into your old age? Everything else in marriage is transitory.
>
> – Friedrich Nietzsche, *Human, All Too Human*

This couple found that the changes that came as they entered later life shunted them out of their familiar world, into harsh and unfamiliar territory. His health difficulties had worsened, since he had started a process of retiring from his work as an academic, and marital difficulties between them had emerged more clearly. When I saw them, the contemporary losses and difficulties were clearly in evidence. He looked much older than her and more depressed. He had had treatment for prostate cancer, a disease he had been advised would not kill him – 'you will die of something else first', he had been told. And indeed, subsequently, he had a stroke, which was not thought to have left him with any cognitive or motor impairment and was presented as 'relatively mild' – a lucky escape. Seeing them together, I was struck by the very different positions they were in – she still relatively young and vital; she was in fact twenty years younger.

Their arguments had increased and had become violent – she complained that he had frightened her for the first time in their married life of over forty years. As they argued in the session, I had a powerful sense of how the fighting, and the state of persecution they were in, functioned to keep at bay the knowledge of the changes in them (particularly, in him) and the losses that faced them. She could, at times, become very contemptuous – look at him, he's useless now. She expressed her anger and bitterness accumulated over years, her earlier sense of abandonment by him in his withdrawal into work and periodic affairs over the lifetime of the marriage – which she had apparently tolerated, but which had become fuel for a powerful grievance felt by her. I had a sense of a complaint that the younger man she had felt deprived of was now not there: and it was too late to get him back. Now he's too old for the other women, he wants me to look after him – this was one of her complaints. And there seemed to be a cruelty and punishment of the other by each of them that became amplified as the losses and changes in them were increasingly inescapable.

Although, by his account, he had always been difficult – a stern patriarch – his behaviour had become much more so. His family told him that they were left on tenterhooks, waiting all the time for his next 'explosion' of temper. When he had had the stroke, and was in hospital, he said, he had been struck by how it was other people who were affected by it – not him; he was only affected indirectly, by their reactions. I thought that he was showing me how he projected his anxiety – his explosions leaving others in the position of never knowing when the next one would strike – like his stroke. These rages were triggered often by evidence of his displacement, from his traditional role as patriarch, the father in charge of the family, and of himself. In the countertransference, I struggled with feelings of wanting to prove my potency as a therapist, in the face of a subtle (and, at times, not so subtle) disparagement of my capacities. I was asked, on a number of occasions, whether I was the right man for the job. I had to bear the projection of being useless, not up to it – impotent and ineffective. I felt frustration, and there was a sense that there was not enough time in the session – that I would not have enough time to prove my abilities.

At one session, they described an argument that they had had. The gardener had been mixing up the rubbish, putting the gardening rubbish not in the green dustbin but in the ordinary household dustbin, which was nearly full, and my patient had had to deal with this himself. The rubbish was then in the 'weekend' bin, which was filled up. The gardener had never known about this criticism, but the patient and his wife had got into an argument about it. I took up how perhaps he felt that I mixed things up inside him, stirring up difficult feelings that they had been left to manage over the weekend break – left to sort out the mess themselves. He often spoke about how I left him to do the talking, and asked whether there would come a time when I would give them something, some advice about what to do. The irony of the issue, he said, was that the gardener knew nothing of this, nothing about his criticism. I thought there was a question of whether I could know about his critical feelings towards me – for not sorting out the mess but leaving him to do it himself – and also, perhaps, his hatred for me, for my thinking, which disturbed the way he had tried to organise things in himself.

When I took this up, he responded: none of us is getting any younger – I am the eldest and older than my wife – but I have had a stroke. Can anything be done? Behind the question of his commitment to me – was I the right man for the job, his cynicism about psychologists – I thought there was a fear about my commitment to them – would I be prepared to stay with them, did I think anything could be done? And would she, his younger wife, stay with him in his old age – his own anxiety about being left was now more evident – which had been projected into her, keeping her at the painful excluded point, of the Oedipal triangle, through his affairs, earlier on. 'Not that I think you are going to get fed up and say there isn't any point in continuing', he went on. 'I do have cynicism about all psychologists – that's my character – I hope you don't feel it too rudely. You show an interest, that gives me hope', but he quickly moved back again to assert his imperviousness – it is other people who feel worried – 'in hospital, they thought I might die – it didn't matter to me, only them, I was out for the count'. He projected his anxieties, and maintained it was other people who were affected, 'I don't suffer'; them, not me. But I felt that this was very thin: I took up how he repeatedly told me that it didn't matter to him, but he did worry about the impact of his criticisms and attacks, it was not true that he was unaffected. For the first time, he was tearful – his daughter and son-in-law had threatened not to see him, not to come on the fiftieth anniversary holiday for the family that he had planned – this was very difficult for him.

The issue of the age difference between them emerged as a painful reality. He had had to go away on business and the plane was delayed, and he had been stranded for several days before being able to get a flight home. She had been left waiting at the airport, and had eventually had to go home and await his return. This separation had brought to mind the thought of his death, of her being left on her own. She said that there was something about his not coming back that had made her think about death. He had spoken to her about his fear of slowing down, which made her think about what was ahead as he got older. At one session, he said he felt faced with the reality of his age by their grandchildren and their demands. He thought that it was to do with not having so much energy that faced him with that, and with things that he found it harder to do as he got older. He had always used his energy to disguise something: the reality of his age, he added. I said that I wondered how much this 'energy' kept away internal realities that he did not want to face, more depressed feelings. He said, 'I get quite panicked and desperate about not having enough time left to do the things I want to do.'

There was a very painful sense of his sadness at growing older and thoughts about how old he would be when their grandchildren were still young. She joined in by saying that she also felt similarly in relation to the competing demands of their domestic life, children and grandchildren, and her career – how much time did she have for this? While I thought this was true, I felt that, at that moment, the more difficult area was the difference between them. When I said this, she commented that the closer she moved towards him, the more she felt like wanting to scream 'I can't stand you'. So, she said, 'I keep a distance, where I can think about things in a more analytic way'. I thought that this might be more pronounced at times like today, when difficult feelings were closer: feelings of depression, the reality of age, and panic at time running out. I wondered if the session moved into 'I can't stand you' in the face of these feelings: a hatred of the reality, with anger as a defence against depression.

Over time, I felt there was some evidence of a shift in their projective system, with her seeming to become more depressed, as he felt better. I said that it was striking that as he got better, she got worse. It seemed that they couldn't both be in a vulnerable, depressed state. She said, yes that was her fear – them both going down at the same time. She spoke then about how, if she got depressed, he would have to look after her. Last week, she had found it difficult to cope, and had needed him to look after her. She'd then started feeling very bad and persecuted for it in her mind, for her weakness. I linked what was happening internally to her – the attacks on her for her vulnerability and need for help, to what was so often enacted between them, in terms of how he was often depressed or vulnerable and she tended to complain about, or attack this, in him. She said, 'I get angry when he doesn't cope, because then I feel everything is falling apart'. Until this point, the pattern had been that she tended to take up the position of being the therapist to him, and distanced herself in this way. He seemed to exploit his vulnerability, milking it, taking up a self-blaming *'mea culpa'* attitude, which also had the effect of distancing the listener. In this way, they seemed to be keeping me at a distance, and one another. I felt that the picture starting to emerge was of a shared unconscious phantasy that intimacy, or closeness, could lead to psychic disaster. This seemed to be expressed by them in terms of a fear of 'both going down together', into depression as I have described. She often exemplified this, in her way of keeping a distance from vulnerability or more infantile feelings, but I also came to feel that, at times, it was manifest in his apparent readiness to be vulnerable, which turned into a readiness to 'take the blame'. I felt that this had an unchanging, repetitive quality that also served to distance him from emotional contact, keeping going a shared pattern between them in which contact was disallowed, or glimpsed but quickly retreated from.

As time went on, more intimate contact might start to develop, but was then withdrawn from. Some way into the therapy, there was a point when the couple were feeling a sense of progress. They came to one session describing this and speaking of how they had taken steps to plan a date for his retirement and a move to the house in the countryside that she had long wanted him to commit to doing. There was a giggly atmosphere in the session as they discussed this, and I wondered to myself whether there was a manic quality. This then changed as he added that this was not only a practical issue: 'I just feel that something's changed in me. I want to make a commitment to her.' There were a number of caveats that then followed. I said how shy he was of these feelings; how they both were, and how difficult to put them into words. He then spoke of feeling childish, foolish to be speaking like this here. I said that there was the sense of him expecting to be shot down, to be attacked. There was then some discussion of the thought of his dying. I felt moved at this point in the session, but also uncertain and a little mistrustful of my feelings. To what extent was all of this a manic flight? Then, he said that he had thought of something and he went into a theoretical account, a kind of discourse on love, and self-deception. His account continued in this vein, and I felt that now a false note was being struck. Although still feeling unsure in the session, my feeling was that his declaration to her had not been self-deception, more that it was now being 'shot down'. I said this to them, and they each agreed. He then said:

> I feel I've faced up to something, which is my own death. I mean, I know this feeling will come and go, but I feel I've faced up to the reality of my own death. I know I have got a lot of facing up to do – including financially – but I feel I have started and it's a relief. I don't want to leave a mess ... I love her.

There was then a shy smile between them, and I felt moved.

Although very difficult to sustain, and followed frequently by retreat, there were nevertheless glimpses with this couple of a struggle to engage in the reality of their present situation, where they were in their lives, and to begin to acknowledge what was ahead.

Conclusion

De Masi (2004) points out the inherently traumatic nature of the prospect of death, for all of us. As Brearley (2005) points out, in the face of trauma, we all need our carapaces – the price of life is a degree of protective 'deadness'. What is at issue is the relative balance of this – the difficulty of 'protections' that destroy the good objects that are needed, most of all, to help the individual to manage this stage of life. It is very difficult to think about ageing and mortality. To paraphrase Prince Siddhartha: how difficult it can be to take delight in life, when we, and all things, must pass away. Where the displacements of old age, and the losses they entail, are too difficult to face, there can be a retreat from the reality of time passing, a migration into the more timeless state of psychic retreat. Rather than knowledge of death and of the finitude of time – which is linked to a capacity to apprehend both – here there is the situation of a retreat from paranoid-schizoid and depressive anxieties, which, as Jacques points out, otherwise shape our perceptions of death, into a state of stasis – a state of mind in which there is no time, and, therefore, in a sense, no death. Perhaps, then, the view of Heidegger and others, in which death is known about, and whereby this knowledge shapes our perception of time, is a developmental achievement. Moving out of the atemporal world of the psychic retreat, perhaps particularly in later life, is a profoundly difficult developmental move.

In the first case I described, particularly earlier in the work with her, very little disturbed the tranquillity of her state, which was also linked to a severance of contact with others and with herself, a psychic retreat, which maintained, for the most part, an ethereal state of timelessness. Although there was a sign of a shift in this, I was left with a sense of the fragility of her emergence from a state of psychic constriction that dominated her life. The second case example described how the couple found the move into later life a profound displacement from their sense of themselves. Although they took refuge in stuck and unmoving states between them, they showed evidence, too, of an apprehension of time passing, linked at moments to a wish to make use of the time that was left.

These states of retreat are not unique to old age. Prince Siddhartha is a young man in a state of renunciation in the face of the facts of life, the inevitability of the losses of ageing, and death. I have younger patients for whom the struggle between renunciation and living is acute, where the state of retreat can feel preferable to the risks of life and intimacy. However, as the realities of ageing impinge more, and the weight of loss builds, there may be problems, particularly when difficulties with earlier loss leave the individual without an internal support for working through the losses of old age. The clinical picture presented here is one in which the inner world situation of earlier object loss, and the contemporary internal legacy of difficulties in facing loss and mourning, join up with the experience in old age of displacement at an individual, and a social, level. In the face of this, we can see how some people become 'internal refugees' migrating to a psychic retreat, in the face of the losses of ageing and impending mortality, as internal and external realities converge. The difficulties are not new: the problems of loss and mourning are ones we all face, from the beginning of our lives, which may become amplified later on. The meaning of loss and mortality may also take on particular qualities, unique to this stage of life – but with their roots in earliest experience. In this sense, perhaps there may be both a crossing into new and foreign territory, while returning to a familiar land.

References

Bell, D. (2006). Existence in Time: Development or Catastrophe. *Psychoanalytic Quarterly*, 75, 783–805.
Birkstead-Breen, D. (2009). 'Reverberation Time', Dreaming and the Capacity to Dream. *International Journal of Psychoanalysis*, 90, 35–51.
Brearley, M. (2005). Review of the Book *Making Death Thinkable* by Franco De Masi. *International Journal of Psychoanalysis*, 86, 1493–1497.
Bromberg, W. and Schilder, P. (1933). Death and Dying: A Comparative Study of the Attitudes and Mental Reactions towards Death and Dying. *Psychoanalytic Review*, 20, 133–185.
Bronstein, C. (2002). Borges, Immortality and the Circular Ruins. *International Journal of Psychoanalysis*, 83, 647–660.
Conrad, J. (1990). *The Shadow Line*. Penguin.
de Beauvoir, S. (1972). *Old Age*. Penguin.
De Masi, F. (2004). *Making Death Thinkable*. Free Association.
Eliot, T. S. (1944). The Dry Salvages. In T. S. Eliot, *Four Quartets*. Faber & Faber.
Feinstein, E. (2007). *Afghan*, in *Talking to the Dead*. Carcanet Press.
Freud, S. (1915). Thoughts for the Time on War and Death. In J. Strachey (ed. and trans.), *The Standard Edition of the Works of Sigmund Freud, Vol. 14*. Hogarth Press.
Freud, S. (1923). The Ego and the Id and Other Works. In J. Strachey (ed. and trans.), *The Standard Edition of the Works of Sigmund Freud, Vol. 19*. Hogarth Press.
Jacques, E. (1965). Death and the Mid-Life Crisis. *International Journal of Psychoanalysis*, 46, 502–514.
Lee, M. (2006). *UK Inquiry into Mental Health and Well-Being in Later Life*. Age Concern and the Mental Health Foundation.
Martindale, B. (1989). Becoming Dependent Again: The Fears of Some Elderly Persons and their Younger Therapists. *Psychoanalytic Psychotherapy*, 4(1), 67–75.

Money-Kyrle, R. (1971). The Aim of Psychoanalysis. *International Journal of Psychoanalysis*, 61, 153–160.

Nietzsche, F. (2024 [1878]). *Human, All Too Human*. Retrieved from https://gutenberg.org/ebooks/38145 (accessed October 2024).

O'Shaughnessy, E. (1981). A Clinical Study of a Defensive Organization. *International Journal of Psychoanalysis*, 62, 359–369.

Quinodoz, D. (2009). Growing Old: A Psychoanalyst's Point of View. *International Journal of Psychoanalysis*, 90, 773–793.

Rack, P. (1982). *Race, Culture and Mental Disorder*. J. W. Arrowsmith.

Reisenberg-Malcolm, R. (1988 [1970]). The Mirror: A Perverse Sexual Phantasy in a Woman as a Defence against Psychotic Breakdown. In E. Bott Spillius (ed.), *Melanie Klein Today, vol. 2: Mainly Practice*. Routledge.

Rosenfeld, H. (1964). On the Psychopathology of Narcissism: A Clinical Approach. *International Journal of Psychoanalysis*, 45, 332–337.

Segal, H. (1984). Joseph Conrad and the Mid-Life Crisis. *International Review of Psycho-Analysis*, 11, 3.

Shepard, A. (1995). *The Prince Who Had Everything: The Legend of the Buddha*. Calliope.

Steiner, J. (1987). The Interplay between Pathological Organizations and the Paranoid-Schizoid and Depressive Positions. *International Journal of Psychoanalysis*, 68, 69–80.

Steiner, J. (1993). *Psychic Retreats*. Routledge.

Thomas, D. (1952). Do Not Go Gentle into that Good Night. In D. Thomas, *In Country Sleep*. New Directions Books.

Thornstam, L. (1997). Gerotranscendence: The Contemplative Dimension of Aging. *Journal of Aging Studies*, 11, 143–154.

Whitehorn, K. (2007). *Selective Memory*. Virago. Bell, D. (2006). Existence in Time: Development or Catastrophe. *Psychoanalytic Quarterly*, 75, 783–805.

Birkstead-Breen, D. (2009). 'Reverberation Time', Dreaming and the Capacity to Dream. *International Journal of Psychoanalysis*, 90, 35–51.

Brearley, M. (2005). Review of the Book *Making Death Thinkable* by Franco De Masi. *International Journal of Psychoanalysis*, 86, 1493–1497.

Bromberg, W. and Schilder, P. (1933). Death and Dying: A Comparative Study of the Attitudes and Mental Reactions towards Death and Dying. *Psychoanalytic Review*, 20, 133–185.

Bronstein, C. (2002). Borges, Immortality and the Circular Ruins. *International Journal of Psychoanalysis*, 83, 647–660.

Conrad, J. (1990). *The Shadow Line*. Penguin.

de Beauvoir, S. (1972). *Old Age*. Penguin.

De Masi, F. (2004). *Making Death Thinkable*. Free Association.

Eliot, T. S. (1944). The Dry Salvages. In T. S. Eliot, *Four Quartets*. Faber & Faber.

Feinstein, E. (2007). *Afghan*, in *Talking to the Dead*. Carcanet Press.

Freud, S. (1915). Thoughts for the Time on War and Death. In J. Strachey (ed. and trans.), *The Standard Edition of the Works of Sigmund Freud, Vol. 14*. Hogarth Press.

Freud, S. (1923). The Ego and the Id and Other Works. In J. Strachey (ed. and trans.), *The Standard Edition of the Works of Sigmund Freud, Vol. 19*. Hogarth Press.

Jacques, E. (1965). Death and the Mid-Life Crisis. *International Journal of Psychoanalysis*, 46, 502–514.

Lee, M. (2006). *UK Inquiry into Mental Health and Well-Being in Later Life*. Age Concern and the Mental Health Foundation.

Martindale, B. (1989). Becoming Dependent Again: The Fears of Some Elderly Persons and their Younger Therapists. *Psychoanalytic Psychotherapy*, 4(1), 67–75.

Money-Kyrle, R. (1971). The Aim of Psychoanalysis. *International Journal of Psychoanalysis*, 61, 153–160.

O'Shaughnessy, E. (1981). A Clinical Study of a Defensive Organization. *International Journal of Psychoanalysis*, 62, 359–369.

Quinodoz, D. (2009). Growing Old: A Psychoanalyst's Point of View. *International Journal of Psychoanalysis*, 90, 773–793.

Rack, P. (1982). *Race, Culture and Mental Disorder*. J. W. Arrowsmith.

Reisenberg-Malcolm, R. (1988 [1970]). The Mirror: A Perverse Sexual Phantasy in a Woman as a Defence against Psychotic Breakdown. In E. Bott Spillius (ed.), *Melanie Klein Today, vol. 2: Mainly Practice*. Routledge.

Rosenfeld, H. (1964). On the Psychopathology of Narcissism: A Clinical Approach. *International Journal of Psychoanalysis*, 45, 332–337.

Segal, H. (1984). Joseph Conrad and the Mid-Life Crisis. *International Review of Psycho-Analysis*, 11, 3.

Shepard, A. (1995). *The Prince Who Had Everything: The Legend of the Buddha*. Calliope.

Steiner, J. (1987). The Interplay between Pathological Organizations and the Paranoid-Schizoid and Depressive Positions. *International Journal of Psychoanalysis*, 68, 69–80.

Steiner, J. (1993). *Psychic Retreats: Pathological, Organizations in Psychotic, Neurotic and Borderline Patients*. Routledge.

Thomas, D. (1952). Do Not Go Gentle into that Good Night. In D. Thomas, *In Country Sleep*. New Directions Books.

Thornstam, L. (1997). Gerotranscendence: The Contemplative Dimension of Aging. *Journal of Aging Studies*, 11, 143–154.

Whitehorn, K. (2007). *Selective Memory*. Virago.

Chapter 4

Thinking about the Experience of Dementia

The Importance of the Unconscious Mind

This chapter explores the challenge of comprehending the experience of dementia and highlights the importance of understanding unconscious processes both at the level of the individual with dementia, and at the level of care-giving relationships in formal and informal settings. The contribution of insights from the research and clinical literature to understanding what may be happening at an unconscious level in dementia care settings is reviewed, and the implications for our understanding of the psychological needs of people with dementia and their carers are discussed.

Dementia affects one in five people over eighty years of age, and with an ageing population, the number of older people living with dementia is set to increase exponentially. While we are faced with the challenge of understanding the experience of the person with dementia, and there is acknowledgement that this is crucial to our understanding of the disease itself (Weiner 1988), the experience of dementia has historically been neglected by researchers. Froggatt (1988) comments that it is difficult to give credence to 'fragmented thought', but that this difficulty has led to the experience of dementia becoming an 'invisible' one. In the history of care for people with dementia, the question of what meaning can be accorded to communication and behaviour as the disease progresses has been a central one (see Kitwood 1988, 1989, 1990a, 1990b; Miessen 1993; Lyman 1989; Fertzinger 1988; Gubrium 1987; Schmid 1990; Bender 2003; Bender and Cheston 1997). We are faced not only with the limits of our current research knowledge of the experience of dementia, but with a challenge to our very capacity to understand what it may be like for a person to move into a world of encroaching incomprehension.

Self-Awareness and Dementia

As awareness of the dementias touches more lives, it has become generally known that they bring continued deterioration of mental functioning, loss of memory and language and increasing difficulty in performing the ordinary tasks of daily life. How can we imagine this? One man in the early stages of dementia, put it like this:

> My mind's boggled, to put it in a rough term ... it's boggled and I can't express myself very straightforwardly as I used to be able to. I have to fight my mind to get it to work, or express a word, to carry what understanding I've got.

He tried to tell me about something else, but lost the words. I asked if this was an example of the feeling of being 'boggled' that he had told me about. He said:

> Yes, yes, I am boggled at it. It's blotchy, blotchy ... it's a feeling that I don't know. Don't know anything about that. I don't want to appear as though I am so far away from everything, and everybody ... it's gone right out, the subject I spoke about ... it's gone right out of my mind.

This man lost his thoughts but was able to talk about what was happening. What about the person who is not able to do so, or who recovers their thoughts, but knows that it will not be an improving picture: they have found them again this time, but next time they may not? Over time, the individual's capacity to convey in words what they are experiencing is lost, and our understanding of what they may be experiencing becomes ever more difficult, as they progress further into dementia.

In Alzheimer's disease, the commonest form of dementia, there is often reported to be a lack of insight, an apparent lack of awareness of what is happening, as the disease progresses. This 'lack of knowledge, awareness or recognition of disease' (McGlynn and Schacter 1989) is known as anosognosia. After many years of neglect, there has recently been increasing research interest in the self-awareness of people with Alzheimer's disease (see Clare 2004b). One reason for this research effort is that anosognosia has important clinical implications. Firstly, unawareness in people with Alzheimer's disease is associated with increased levels of burden experienced by caregivers (Seltzer, Vasterling, Yoder, and Thompson 1997; DeBettingies, Mahurin, and Pirozzolo 1990). Secondly, such research promises to inform how the needs of affected individuals are conceptualised: increased understanding of the experience of the person with Alzheimer's disease is a prerequisite for improving the quality and responsiveness of services (Clare 2004b; Froggatt 1988). Post (1995) points out that, if someone is considered to be unaware, this has negative implications for the kind of treatment that they will receive.

There are many assessment tools for determining the presence or absence of insight. However, these have been restricted to assessments of conscious expressions of awareness. This way of thinking about self-awareness does not have a place for the unconscious mind, for the existence of non-conscious awareness in people with dementia, despite a number of reports suggesting the importance of this dimension of awareness (McGlynn and Schacter

1989). In recent years, there has been more research into the experience of dementia (Clare 2004a, 2004b), and the current state of our knowledge suggests that at least in many cases, the early stages are characterized by an extremely painful awareness of the situation. In an exploratory interview that I conducted with a man in the earlier stages of Alzheimer's disease, Mr A, he showed a high degree of insight into his problems, acknowledging his difficulties:

> I need to feel better than I am mind-wise. When it stared to get me, I wouldn't believe it. It started when I was in the shed. I put a hammer down and wondered where it was gone. It wasn't clicking there [indicates head] like it ought to. When I went to remember where it was there was a kind of blank.

In response to a question about what this feeling of blankness was like, he said: 'It is nauseating really. My wife says, "Stop and think a little while." I say, "It's stopping and thinking that's worrying me, because there ain't nothing coming back from the thinking."' He then distanced himself from this, saying, 'Normally I am quite OK. But there was a time when it seemed there was a blankness.'

He went on to describe his experience as a child, and having problems with his ear and being 'poked about with'. The doctors, however, couldn't actually do anything to help him. When I said that he might also be telling me about his experience now, he said, 'Yes, the bit that hurts you really, is that you know in your mind's eye that you are not a symptom, but in my actions I feel that I am, you know.'

In later-stage dementia, it is harder to learn directly from conscious, verbal accounts of people's experiences. A neurologist, writing in a guide for carers published on the internet, comments that people in later-stage dementia appear to have no awareness of what is happening to them, and therefore it is really the carers that he feels sorry for. Is there simply the shell of a person, physically intact but psychically empty by the end of the disease process? Richard Eyre, former director of the National Theatre, writing about his experience of his mother when she had Alzheimer's disease, states that 'The personality starts to disappear, and with it the humanity and soul, leaving as if in mockery only the body to breathe and be fed' (*The Times*, 3 June 1996).

Others have written of the need to be careful about making assumptions about the absence of awareness in later stage dementia, given the limits of our current knowledge and the risk of underestimating remaining capacities. Indeed, recent research (Phinney 2002) points out that awareness is not an all or nothing phenomenon, there can be different levels of awareness, and awareness can fluctuate over time. What might remain, at an unconscious level of the experiences of people with dementia, whether or not they are consciously able to articulate them? An exploratory study (Balfour 1995) aimed to assess evidence of awareness in individuals across the range of disability, including people in the later stages of dementia. Pictures from the Thematic Apperception Test (Murray 1943) were shown to participants who were asked to describe what they saw. The approach of using pictures to stimulate responses arose from initial difficulties that were encountered in asking people with dementia, particularly those whose dementia was more advanced, questions about their experience. This approach was found to elicit relevant responses even in some people who were in the advanced stages of dementia, providing that attention was paid to 'snatches' of lucidity in otherwise disconnected narratives. A group of individuals with dementia gave responses that featured a preoccupation with damage and disability when they were shown a picture of a boy contemplating a violin on a table in front of him (a matched control group who had no cognitive impairment, did not make reference to this theme). One remarked, 'There are tears in the violin. He is not very keen on the violin. He has probably been practising it and it hasn't gone quite right ... He's in despair over his violin.' Another: 'He looks blind. There is something wrong with him ... I don't know whether he thinks at all, he is thinking about the violin and wishing for better health.' Another person, also at a later stage of dementia, commented: 'It's a boy. He's got a violin ... He's gone deaf, very deaf. Gone very deaf. He is playing the violin, he's gone very deaf.' Finally: 'He's in despair over his violin, he can't get it to do the thing he wants. He's despondent about what he's been able to take in.'

Whether or not insight is retained, a psychodynamic understanding would be that anxieties are felt at both conscious and also at unconscious levels. Disturbing states of mind, and unconscious fears or anxieties, may be experienced by individuals with dementia at other stages, not only early on in the illness, when fears may be more easily put into words. In this regard, the quality of care giving, including the psychological as well as the physical dimensions of care, remains of crucial importance throughout.

The Clinical Setting

In the clinical setting, how might we try to think about the internal experience of the person in the later stages of dementia? To give an example from a case discussion group, a psychiatrist working in a multi-disciplinary team described a referral of a patient whom staff in a residential setting had been finding increasingly difficult to manage. This patient, an elderly woman whom I shall call Mrs Brown, had made a number of accusations about thefts from her room. Each time, there had been some investigation, but no evidence of any actual theft was found. In any case, staff were used to this: it was not an uncommon complaint from residents that things were going missing, or being taken from them. On one occasion, she had become very distressed indeed, about the perceived theft of a calendar. She also regularly complained that the TV and the remote control were not working properly.

Staff would respond wearily to familiar complaints that they felt were to do with their resident's cognitive impairment, her loss of judgement and understanding.

When the psychiatrist involved found out more history, from colleagues who had also been involved in her care, he learnt about what had led to her residential placement. She had been seen by them, some months earlier, when she had complained about intruders who, she believed, had moved in to the upstairs part of her house. For some time, Mrs Brown had not seemed to be too disturbed by this delusion, and was managing at home. However, she said that she did not like their intrusive noise, and things had worsened for her when, she believed, the intruders had brought a little child to live with them, who cried in distress at night. One day, living at home, she had had a fall. She had lain on the floor for several hours before help came. When the doctor interviewed her, she had complained bitterly that these intruders, who she had tolerated for so long, had not offered her any help when she was on the floor and unable to get up, or raise help. It was this incident that had led to her leaving her home and moving into residential care.

The psychiatrist learned that a little time before the development of her delusion about the 'intruders' moving in, she had lost her husband of many years. She had suffered from dementia for some time, and he had looked after her at their home. What had been striking at the time was how she experienced his death. She became convinced that he was not dead at all; he was alive, but he was seeing another woman instead of her. Although the evidence was that he had been faithful to her throughout a long-married life, her husband's absence was filled by the preoccupation that he was off having an affair. She expressed anger and betrayal; he was not gone but was actively withholding himself from her and excluding her by being with someone else. Instead of experiencing the loss as absence, it was filled with persecuting thoughts, to do with exclusion and betrayal, anxieties that may be linked to our earliest experiences, encountered in our first relationships. She remained for some time at home, living, as far as she was concerned, with 'the intruders'. After her fall, her concerned family felt that she was no longer able to live at home, and she was moved into residential care. It was, in many ways, a nice place, well equipped, and modern. But it was not her home. Without her familiar bearings, she seemed quickly to grow more confused. Waking up in the night, unsure of her surroundings, she tended to wander the corridors. In confusion and frustration, angry and lost, deserted by her familiar objects, both external and internal ones, she smashed things – possibly conveying the violent shattering of her internal world that she was experiencing. Wandering up and down, and pacing, are common in extreme states of grief, or agitation and loss. For her, an internal dislocation was met by the actual displacement of being moved out of a familiar environment. This is likely to be very important indeed – as her internal experience was of moving into states of unknowing and confusion and now her external environment known for so many years had gone too. External reality overlapped internal experience in such a way as to dramatically throw her capacity to find any bearings. Shortly after her admission, she again had a fall.

We can only guess at what the experience is like for this woman, whose ego functioning (in psychodynamic terms, the executive functioning of the mind to do with memory, perception, and judgement) is diminished, whose conscious sense of time passing, of knowing that certain predictable things happen at predictable times and can be anticipated, is lost. So, although her family visited every Saturday, she complained bitterly that she was completely abandoned and left alone. Lacking fixed reference points, the knowledge about a future visit to hold onto, she may have experienced a sense of endless, timeless, abandonment, left alone, in unbearable states of mind with little internal or external support.

Are Mrs Brown's complaints and delusional beliefs to be seen only as the product of a diseased mind, and symptomatic only of organic deterioration? A psychodynamic approach would suggest otherwise and in understanding aspects of her internal experience we can see the way in which her psychiatrist was able to digest and make sense of that which could not be articulated at a conscious level. Her husband's death seems to have been linked to a further break down in her capacities, with the development of her delusional beliefs about a co-habiting intruder, living 'upstairs'. This may convey the breaking through 'upstairs', in her mind, of intrusive and disturbing thoughts. The situation became even more intolerable for her when she felt she was confronted by the intruders' distressed young child, which might express the distressed infantile part of her, now breaking through. The trauma of her fall, and the experience of lying on the ground without help for some time was vividly conveyed in her sense of abandonment; her bitter complaint that the intruders who lived in the house did nothing to help her. In terms of her internal experience she makes it clear that she has been abandoned by good and helpful internal figures and left in the hands of bad and persecuting ones responsible for the experience of loss and trauma.

Mrs Brown's mental and physical deterioration seems to return her to earlier, problematic emotional constellations, which may increasingly dominate her mind. Once in the residential home Mrs Brown wanders at night, occasionally smashing things. At such times, relatives feel that she is a long way from being the shy and sensitive woman, concerned to behave politely, that she had always been. Her accusations of theft of money, and of her calendar, and complaints about the non-functioning TV, resulted in a lot of staff activity, in having to check that things hadn't in reality been stolen. Possibly, this conveys that what internally gave her a sense of order, symbolised by the loss of her calendar, is gone; as one capacity after another is lost. Accusations of theft are not unusual in this setting and the staff were weary of hearing them. Frustrating as it was for staff to be on the receiving end of this again and again, it might be helpful if they had a forum in which the link could be made that these may not simply be misguided complaints of people whose cognitive impairments make them unable to judge what is happening. These accusations may convey how one capacity after another is being taken from Mrs Brown, and how persecutory is the quality of the losses involved. How she may feel that parts of herself, of her functioning mind, are being stolen from her, and that she is left, like the TV, not working properly.

Long unresolved psychological difficulties often re-emerge and determine the way in which losses and changes are experienced in later life. For the individual with dementia, the ego's resources and defences are progressively diminished and less available, and so emotional difficulties may develop, such as depression, anxiety, paranoid states, and in the later stages, these may take a psychotic, delusional form. Our current understanding is that earlier problematic emotional constellations do not 'grow old' in the sense of diminishing or fading away but persist and become more powerful as dependency increases and adult coping falls away, 'because the unconscious does not participate in the process of growing older' (Grotjahn 1940). Miessen (1993) makes the poignant observation that many people in the more advanced stages of dementia experience the delusion that their parents are alive, what he terms the phenomenon of 'parent fixation'. In a fictional account, Ian McEwan describes a younger man visiting his mother, who has dementia, in an institutional setting. His mother, Lily, says 'I'm waiting to go home. I'm getting the bus.' The narrative continues:

> It pains him whenever she says that, even though he knows she's referring to her childhood home where she thinks her mother is waiting for her ... Lily says: 'I was there last week ... on the bus and my mum was in the garden. I said to her, You can walk down there, see what you're going to get and the next thing is the balancing of everything you've got. She's not well. Her feet. I'll go along there in a minute and I can't help losing her a jersey.' How strange it would have been for Lily's mother, an aloof, unmaternal woman, to have known that the little girl at her skirts would one day, in a remote future, a science fiction date in the next century, talk of her all the time and long to be home with her. Would that have softened her? Now Lily is set, she'll talk for as long as he sits there. It's hard to tell if she's actually happy. Sometimes she laughs, at others she describes shadowy disputes and grievances, and her voice becomes indignant ...
>
> (McEwan 2005, pp. 162–163)

At the other end of the lifespan, as Fraiberg et al. (1975) point out, the infant's psychological legacy will in part be determined by the unresolved emotional issues of the parents, and this is evocatively described as the presence of 'ghosts in the nursery': 'visitors from the unremembered pasts of the parents; the uninvited guests at the christening...the intruders...may break through...taking up residence in the nursery claiming tradition and rights of ownership.' At the other end of life, in dementia, we see how there can be a breaking through of earlier unresolved emotional constellations, appearing now as phantoms in the mind, the return of the long-ago- ghosts of the nursery. Current experience, even in the profound psychic disruptions of dementia, is shaped and coloured by earlier times, and even the unremembered past may now make its presence felt as 'ghosts' in the care setting.

Relationships with Carers

The more a mind is lost, the more it falls to the carers of people with dementia to provide a thinking mind, a container for their increasingly fragmented experience. Here there is an ongoing task: 'to struggle to translate and make sense of the individual's distressed and bizarre communications, often conveyed through projective identification which may replace ordinary language.' (Davenhill 1998). Increasingly the carer becomes the witness, the mind that might think and register what is happening to the person whose own capacities are progressively eroded. Waddell (2000) describes the importance of this, how the containing function of the carer's capacity to take in and unconsciously register and reflect can give meaning to the world of the person with dementia, and this is conveyed through the caregiver's capacity to care responsively: 'Care of the very elderly, those so often lacking the capacity to speak, yet so intensely riven by extreme emotional states, requires a painful reversal of the original pattern of container-contained (the young now struggling to offer ... [containment] to the old).'

The care of elderly people with dementia is largely undertaken by relatives. According to Carers UK (2024), there are nearly six million carers in the UK looking after someone who is ill or disabled, one million of whom provide 50 hours a week or more, of care. Many of these are husbands or wives. In such relationships, where one partner has dementia, a painful shift may be required, with the burden of containment now falling increasingly on the shoulders of the other partner as the disease progresses. As the American novelist Jonathan Franzen puts it, writing about his own family:

> For my mother, the losses of Alzheimer's both amplified and reversed long-standing patterns in her marriage. My father had always refused to open himself to her, and now increasingly, he couldn't open himself ... living with a man who mistook her for her mother, forgot every fact he had ever known about her and finally ceased to speak her name. He who had always insisted on being the boss in the marriage, the maker of decisions, the adult protector of the childlike wife, couldn't help behaving like the child ... Task by task, she slowly took over their life.
>
> (Jonathan Franzen, *The Guardian*, 15 December 2001)

Research and clinical evidence indicate how important the environment of care giving and the relational world of the individual with dementia are (Pratt and Wilkinson 2003; Clare and Shakespeare 2004). There is evidence that the maintenance of the person with dementia in the community has more to do with the attitudes and well-being of the spouse carer than factors such as severity of the disease itself. Indeed, the tremendous importance of the quality of the care giving relationship is underscored by the finding that low levels of interaction between the partners in the marriages of people with dementia predict the move to hospital care, and even the mortality of the individual with dementia two years later (Wright 1991, 1994). This has powerful implications and shows the clinical significance of work that aims to support and provide containment for carers.

In the interview with Mr A that I described earlier, he went on to convey the importance for him of the containing function of the relationship with his wife. During the interview, while expressing his fears of what it meant that he now attended the 'nut hatch' (the local day hospital, situated in a psychiatric hospital), he expressed his sense that his family might lose him: 'I said to my missus, "I am going to the nut hatch, you are going to lose me." She cried her eyes out and said, "Don't talk like that."'

He conveyed his need of his wife. Her role in serving as a memory aid, as a reassurance of his continuance and maintenance of identity, was eloquently expressed by him. For example:

> My wife will come back with what I've lost ... then I'll carry on because I know I mustn't let it get hold of me ... I've got a good wife and she's a good thinker for me. I feel dodgy sometimes that I should be like I am, that she has to suffer, but she says, 'I don't suffer you, you are the same old C. that I married years ago.' She says, 'You're the same one ...' Well, that helps me.

It is important to recognise the tremendous challenge that this can present for the carer, and the importance of not glossing over or idealising what is possible. This draws our attention to the importance of the state of mind of the carer, and their need for support and containment. What do we know of the experience of providers of care, often husbands or wives, sons or daughters? Carers may have all kinds of feelings towards the individual with dementia in their care, apart from compassionate ones, such as disgust or revulsion, resentment or hatred. Such feelings might arouse tremendous guilt or anxiety, and there may be a great need for help and containment with this. Responses made by carers when asked to tell the story that they thought might underlie pictures presented to them from the Thematic Apperception Test (described earlier) convey this vividly. Describing a picture showing a man and a woman together, one man said:

She's looking for the door and sees that her husband is slumped in the chair and to all intents and purposes has departed this world. She is just dusting and thinking, 'a woman's lot is never done'. I can endorse that, having had to do everything for my wife for a couple of years.

A woman whose husband was in the later stages of dementia said:

> Her husband has been an invalid for the last four years and she's nursed him for three years and he's been dead for three years. This is the first man since to ask her to marry him. She is not sure about another commitment that may turn out to be a burden in years to come. Or else, she just said, 'I've been married for thirty years, and I've just got fed up and put arsenic in your tea.' [Claps hands]

Another woman, whose husband with dementia had recently had a fall, commented:

> I don't know if someone is ill, possibly she's afraid or shocked because of what she's seen. It could be someone is ill on the floor. It is an illness or something. I think she will end up very shaken. And if she has seen something which upset her, she won't forget it.

If we pause to imagine what it may be like for a husband, wife, or other family member to witness the changes wrought by dementia, possibly no longer even being recognised any more by their loved one, we are faced with just how difficult the task of sustaining emotional contact can be under such circumstances. Having emotional contact with fragmented experience is very difficult, and it is understandable that carers who are themselves less contained may be less able to tolerate emotional contact with the person with dementia. Carers need considerable support and containment in order to be able to provide containment for those in their care. The importance of trying to provide carers with this is underlined by our knowledge that whether people with dementia go into institutional care or not and even how long they live, is linked to the quality of their relationship with their carers, which is itself affected by factors such as carer strain. While there is a great deal of publicity now in terms of the needs of mothers with newborn babies for help and support early on in combating post-natal depression, there is relatively little media interest in the needs of the caring relationship at the other end of the lifespan. In the situation of caring for someone with dementia, this might be informal support from the wider family or social network, or formal support from statutory services. The key issue here is the recognition of the importance of the relationship between the person with dementia and their carer. The 'unit of care' may be the husband or wife with a spouse with dementia, or the son or daughter with a parent, or other family members.

When thinking about the enormous emotional and physical demands within the caring relationship we can see how remarkable it is that care of great quality does go on. Many such relationships survive for a long time, enabling the person with dementia to remain out of institutional care and in their familiar environment. This area is extremely important in terms of thinking of the future demands likely to be faced in increasing numbers by older couples and families. In the work of Bowlby (1969, 1973); Robertson and Robertson (1967–1971); Menzies (1988 [1973]), and others, on the care of children in institutional settings, their studies of the attachment needs of children in these circumstances led to a sea change of attitudes. There was a new perception that the 'unit of care' was no longer the child in isolation, but the child and his mother or the family with its child patient. This was reflected in moves within health and social policy towards the view that they should be cared for together, and as a whole. This has clear implications for a similar shift at the other end of life, where the most crucial 'units of care' may be the couple where one partner has a dementia, or the family looking after someone with dementia.

Unconscious Processes within the Dementia Care Setting

Individuals with dementia at the more advanced stages are less able to communicate with language, and staff in contact with them are faced with patients whose inner states are increasingly conveyed through projective processes. An account by the poet Tony Harrison describing a visit to a day hospital for people with dementia conveys something of the quality of the anxiety of close contact with such frailty and diminished capacities:

> You recoil at their clutching, momentarily in ignorant fear that somehow it might transfer their terrible confusion to you. You fear too that their disabled personality might be so fragile that a false move, the wrong physical contact, could make what little control they have disintegrate before you creating some horrendous embarrassment.
> (Tony Harrison, *The Guardian*, 20 August 2005)

The importance and value of psychotherapeutic approaches to service-level interventions with staff working with people with dementia is highlighted by a number of studies. Arden, Garner, and Porter (1998) describe the value of psychotherapeutic input to the old age psychiatry team, as do Stern and Lovestone (2000). Holman and Jackson (2001) describe reflective practice groups for staff on a continuing care ward, based on a psychotherapeutic approach. Ashburner and colleagues describe an evaluation of psychotherapeutically informed clinical supervision for hospital nurses (Ashburner et al 2004a). The same authors describe an action research project aiming to support staff in a continuing care setting, using a psychotherapeutically informed approach (Ashburner et al. 2004b). Davenhill (1998) uses a psychotherapeutic approach to understand the difficulties arising in the provision of long-term care for people with dementia and the institutional and service level response. A number of authors have described the use of psychodynamic observational methods and psychotherapeutic models to understanding issues arising at an institutional level in dementia care settings (e.g. Davenhill et al. 2003; Mackenzie-Smith 1992). Terry (1997) describes work with key workers, care staff and service managers based on psychotherapeutic principles. The work of Kitwood (1997) and Kitwood and Bredin (1994) has had a profound influence in establishing person-centred care based on psychotherapeutic principles. This is exemplified in the now widely used approach of 'dementia care mapping', which aims to provide a systematic method of gaining insight into the quality of care offered in dementia care settings.

An account of a recent, difficult experience was presented in a staff supervision group in a hospital setting. The staff described how there had been an investigation, after a patient had 'wandered' off the unit at night-time, and was missing for 24 hours, before he was found. This had been a traumatic experience for them, and they had spent an anxious day or so, waiting for news. The ensuing investigation started to have the atmosphere of a witch- hunt, as an initial mood of guilt and concern seemed to give way to a culture of blame. The case discussion group, which involved a large, multidisciplinary group of staff, became increasingly heated. They were normally very thoughtful, but accusations began to fly, with comments to the effect that there were some staff who were too negligent, who did not really bother themselves with patients. Before long, there were similar comments, to the effect that others in the team were too intrusive or controlling of patients. These accusations were not exactly personal, in so far as individuals did not name other individuals. Initially, in fact, the targets of the comments were unclear, they were kept as more or less impersonal observations. Gradually, however, it was *nursing staff* who behaved in this way, or *care managers* or *doctors* who behaved in that way. Soon, it became clear that it was the different professional groups who became the identified targets. At one point, there was a comment that a patient had been virtually 'strapped down' to keep them quiet; at other points staff were said to be too busy, and so were neglectful of the patients. One person commented that some staff were too busy ever to think about the minds of their patients. As the consultant to the group, I felt similarly 'strapped down', metaphorically speaking, constrained in terms of what could freely be put into words, and I found it very difficult to think. Complaints were also made about the 'mayhem' that periodically erupted on the ward.

Later, after the meeting, I became interested in their use of this word 'mayhem', and I looked it up. Among other definitions, Collins dictionary offers, 'violent maiming'. This seemed to convey the violent attack upon psychic movement, on freedom of thought, the 'maiming' of the capacity to think and reflect in this atmosphere. Within the group, I had started to feel increasingly hopeless about making any improvement in what was happening in the room, as every avenue seemed to be shot down. After a while, it did become possible to think about whether these were some of the feelings that were difficult to face, feelings of hopelessness in the staff group, the sense that whatever they did, made little difference. In terms of repair, or cure for their patients, the situation was indeed hopeless. Often, their own feelings were turned away from, and projected into the 'mindless' organisation they claimed to work in, which they often attacked in this way. They described the tremendous painfulness of the work, that good work often meant helping people to die. There was the sense of their potentially being overwhelmed by something deathly, reflected in the 'dying institution, decaying NHS', which they often referred to: 'people come here to die ... it's a death sentence. They come in alive, and they leave dead.'

The staff conveyed the sense that if they found words for their feelings, there was a fear of what would emerge, particularly negative feelings rather than compassionate ones. We may be drawn to this area of work in part because of an internal, unconscious motivation to repair damage. In situations where there is no hope of cure, and where the situation is one of progressive deterioration, as in dementia, the failure of such reparative wishes may be hard to bear. The primitive, persecutory guilt that can be felt by staff in such circumstances is very powerful and can be projected around the system. The persecutory elements of their experience were split off and projected into different, rival professional groups. The other groups became the lodging point for feelings that were unbearable for individual staff members to know about in themselves. One of the consequences was that staff showed an increasing division of labour, at a point where there was a need for more integration within the service, and a preoccupation with disputes within the multi-professional team over issues of role and identity. In such conditions, the emotional atmosphere of the care setting became one of schism and fragmentation, at worst a malignant mirroring of the internal fragmentation of the individuals with dementia in their care.

Two features of the descriptions of life on the unit stood out: the 'mayhem' that periodically erupted, which was linked to the 'too-busyness' of the staff to think about the minds of their patients. This might describe what can happen within professionals who are dealing with people who are experiencing such profound loss: a maiming of the capacity to think, and a retreat into 'busy-ness' which avoids a direct contact with such disturbed states of mind. If we consider the level of anxiety that may be felt by such patients, and projected into the professionals involved, we can see how it may lead to fragmentation of thinking in them, mayhem so to speak, and strongly negative feelings may be felt towards those in their care. If this is not contained, if professionals do not have a forum for thinking about such experience, then important sources of information about the patients' state of mind may be neglected and there is the danger that such feelings may be acted out by staff, with all the risks that go along with this. As Obholzer (2000, p. ix) puts it, in such settings, staff go about their daily work 'irradiated with distress'. Without containment and support, they can find themselves acting in ways that echo the difficulties of their patients. In this way the emotional world of older people with dementia can 'infect' those around them, creating a parallel emotional process that, particularly in less contained settings, may be mirrored and enacted by staff.

The author and colleagues (Davenhill et al. 2003) presented an account of observational studies in old age care settings. One of these observations involved a nurse struggling to help an elderly woman, who seemed to be in a lot of pain. The nurse was, for a while, at a loss to know how to help. Her patient was in distress and the nurse tried to give her various things to help her. Nothing she did seemed to help. As described in the observation, at that moment, her patient experienced her own body as a source of persecution to her. One could imagine, aching bones and too thin limbs and her cries suggested that she wanted some unmanageable, painful experience to be taken away. When the nurse tried to give her things, the nurse herself seemed to become experienced as the source of persecution to the patient. An uncomfortable position for her to be in, she looked around for help. She was faced with an empty desk, an observation point, in the centre of the room. If it had been staffed, someone could have come over to help. A supportive extra eye was needed but was not there. Throughout the weeks of the observation, it was always unstaffed, and so perhaps represented the defence, expressed at an institutional level, of turning a blind eye, a maiming, one might say, of the capacity to see or take in. The nurse was not helped, at the most basic level, to tolerate the experience and to stay involved, which might have been possible had there been a third person around. She withdrew for a time, but to her credit, managed later to return to the scene and continued to try to help her patient. This highlights the important question of who is there to contain the container. To draw an analogy with the care of children, a helpful third, an observing eye, is needed to support the nursing couple. In this example, no one is available to help the nurse to contain her patient.

What kind of eye is kept by the hospital on this patient and what can the carer allow themselves to take in? I have tried to capture the difficulty there can be in tolerating a relationship to such losses and diminished functioning. Too often, the most difficult work, in terms of emotional demands, is also the most devalued and unsupported work, and carers of people with dementia remain, in the words of one researcher, 'hidden patients' (Fengler and Goodrich 1979). It is very difficult to witness the losses and take in the experience of people in the later stages of dementia without being overtaken by mayhem, or the maiming of our capacity to think and reflect. None of us is immune from the difficulty of maintaining an emotional engagement and a capacity to think, in such circumstances.

I have described the contribution that thinking about unconscious processes can make in attempting to understand the anxieties and states of mind of the individual with dementia; the partner other family member or friend, and the care giving team in organisational settings. I have tried to show how important, at all these levels, such attempts at understanding are, when the internal situation of the individual with dementia is an inexorable move towards loss of understanding. This is profoundly painful to witness; and the challenges facing carers, in maintaining an emotional availability in such circumstances, cannot be underestimated. Both clinical experience and research, indicate the crucial importance of 'containing the container', the importance of providing the opportunity for carers to process and think about their experience, in order that they are, in turn, helped to take in and think about the experience of those in their care.

There follows a summary of key points and the clinical issues arising from them.

Conclusion

The longstanding neglect of research interest into self-awareness in people with dementia has recently begun to be addressed, though for the most part, has been restricted to conscious expressions of awareness. In order to evolve new treatment approaches, we need to understand better what anxieties and levels of awareness may be retained as dementia progresses. A psychodynamic approach would emphasise the importance of unconscious anxieties persisting, whether or not these can be consciously thought about, or put into words.

As dementia progresses, the individual is less able to articulate their experiences and feelings, which may increasingly be communicated by projective processes. An understanding of such unconscious processes is important in trying to understand the experience of the person with dementia, as well as the experience of carers in close contact with them.

Research and clinical evidence indicate the importance of the relationship with carers, and the quality of such relationships is also affected by factors like carer strain. This has implications for the well-being and even the survival of the person with dementia. Family carers may themselves need considerable help and containment, in particular, the opportunity to think about and have support with the difficult feelings that may be an inevitable part of their experience. Support and containment for carers has relevance in terms of economics, family breakdown (institutional versus community care) and even mortality rates of people with dementia.

Both clinical experience and observational research indicate the importance of seeking to understand the unconscious anxieties and defences that arise in the dementia care setting. Front-line staff are subject to powerful and disturbing projections. It is important that they are given the opportunity to process and discuss the feelings that are engendered in them by working in close contact with such frailty and diminished functioning. Such support and containment for staff is important in helping them to be alongside and emotionally engaged with the people in their care.

Anxieties and defences are expressed at the institutional level, within groups of staff across the dementia care setting. Defences and ways of managing anxieties arising from the difficult work of caring for people with dementia are necessary. However, if staff working at the front line of dementia care are not helped to process the feelings inevitably arising from their work, there is a danger that such feelings will be expressed in ways that negatively affect the quality of care.

Having the opportunity to express difficult emotions arising from such painful work can be challenging and difficult for staff teams. In some organisations this approach can feel to be counter to the prevailing culture. Resistance to it can be met at individual and organisational levels. This is understandable, because it may disrupt the established modes of defence within the organisation, and so, although staff may at an intellectual level agree that such an approach would be a good thing, at another level there may be considerable anxieties about it. It may help to sustain the clinician who wishes to establish such a change within the organisation, to understand what underlies these resistances. Given this, it is also important, when trying to establish this work with staff, that there is support for it at an appropriately senior level within the organisation.

References

Arden, M., Garner, J., and Porter, R. (1998). Curious Bedfellows: Psychoanalytic Understanding and Old Age Psychiatry. *Psychoanalytic Psychotherapy*, 12, 47–56.

Ashburner, C., Meyer, J., Cotter, A., Young, G., and Ansell, R. (2004a). Seeing Things Differently: Evaluating Psychodynamically Informed Group Clinical Supervision for General Hospital Nurses. *Journal of Research in Nursing*, 9(1), 38–48.

Ashburner, C., Meyer, J., Johnson, B., and Smith, C. (2004b). Using Action Research to Address Loss of Personhood in a Continuing Care Setting. *Illness, Crisis and Loss*, 12, 23–37.

Balfour, A. W. (1995). Account of a Study Aiming to Explore the Experience of Dementia. *Psychologists' Special Interest Group in the Elderly Newsletter*, 53, 15–19.

Bender, M. (2003). *Explorations in Dementia: Theoretical and Research Studies into the Experience of Remediable and Enduring Cognitive Losses*. Jessica Kingsley.

Bender, M. P. and Cheston, R. (1997). Inhabitants of a Lost Kingdom: A Model of the Subjective Experiences of Dementia. *Ageing and Society*, 17, 513–532.

Bowlby, J. (1969). *Attachment and Loss, vol 1: Attachment*. Hogarth Press.

Bowlby, J. (1973). *Attachment and Loss, vol 2: Separation – Anxiety and Anger*. Hogarth Press.

Brooker, D. (2004). What Is Person Centred Care for People with Dementia? *Reviews in Clinical Gerontology*, 13(3).

Brooker, D., Edwards, D., and Benson, S. (eds). (2004). *Dementia Care Mapping, Experiences and Insights into Practice*. Hawker Publications.

Cantor, M. H. (1983). Strain among Caregivers. *The Gerontologist*, 23, 597–604.

Carers UK. (2024). Key Facts and Figures about Caring. Retrieved from www.carersuk.org/policy-and-research/key-facts-and-figures (accessed October 2024).

Clare, L. (2004a). Cognitive Training and Cognitive Rehabilitation in Early-Stage Alzheimer's Disease. *Neuropsychological Rehabilitation*.

Clare, L. (2004b). Awareness in Early-Stage Alzheimer's Disease: A Review of Methods and Evidence. *British Journal of Clinical Psychology*, 43, 177–196.

Clare, L. and Shakespeare, P. (2004). Negotiating the Impact of Forgetting: Dimensions of Resistance in Task-Oriented Conversations between People with Early-Stage Dementia and their Partners. *Dementia*, 3, 211–232.

Davenhill, R. (1998). No Truce with the Furies. *Journal of Social Work Practice*, 12 (2), 149–157.

Davenhill, R., Balfour, A., Rustin, M., Blanchard, M., and Tress, K. (2003). Looking into Later Life: Psychodynamic Observation and Old Age. *Psychoanalytic Psychotherapy*, 17, 253–266.

DeBettignies, B. H., Mahurin, R. K., and Pirozzolo, F. J. (1990). Insight for Impairment in Independent Living Skills in Alzheimer's Disease and Multi-infarct Dementia. *Journal of Clinical and Experimental Neuropsychology*, 12, 355–363.

Fengler, A. P. and Goodrich, N. (1979). Wives of Elderly Disabled Men: The Hidden Patients. *The Gerontologist*, 19, 175–183.

Fertzinger, M. (1988). Alzheimer's Disease and the Mind/Body Problem. In R. Mayeaux*et al.* (eds), *Alzheimer's Disease and Related Disorders*. Charles C. Thomas.

Fonagy, P., Steele, M., Moran, G., Steele, H., and Higgitt, A. (1993). Measuring the Ghost in the Nursery: An Empirical Study of the Relation between Parents' Mental Representations of Childhood Experiences and Their Infants' Security of Attachment. *Journal of the American Psychoanalytic Association*, 41, 957–989.

Fraiberg, S., Adelson, E., and Shapiro, V. (1975). Ghosts in the Nursery: A Psychoanalytic Approach to the Problem of Impaired Mother Infant Relationships. *Journal of the American Academy of Child & Adolescent Psychiatry*, 14, 387–422.

Froggatt, A. (1988). Self Awareness in Early Dementia. In B. Gearing, M. Johnson, and T. Heller (eds), *Mental Health Problems in Old Age*. Wiley.

Frampton, M. (2004). Experience Assessment and Management of Pain in People with Dementia. *Age and Ageing*, 32, 248–251.

Garner, J. (1997). An Intimate Death. *British Journal of Medical Psychology*, 70, 177–184.

Garner, J. (2004). Dementia. In S. Evans and J. Garner (eds), *Talking Over the Years*. Brunner-Routledge.

Gubrium, J. S. (1987). Structuring and Destructuring the Course of Illness: The Alzheimer's Disease Experience. *Sociology of Health and Illness*, 9(1), 1–24.

Grotjahn, M. (1940). Psychoanalytic Investigation of a Seventy-One Year Old Man with Senile Dementia. *Psychoanalytic Quarterly*, 9, 80–97.

Holman, C. and Jackson, S. (2001). A Team Education Project: An Evaluation of a Collaborative Education and Practice Development in a Continuing Care Unit for Older People. *Nurse Education Today*, 21, 97–103.

Kitwood, T. (1988). The Contribution of Psychology to the Understanding of Dementia. In B. Gearing, M. Johnson, and T. Heller (eds), *Mental Health Problems in Old Age*. Wiley.

Kitwood, T. (1989). Brain, Mind and Dementia, with Particular Reference to Alzheimer's Disease. *Ageing and Society*, 10.

Kitwood, T. (1990a). Understanding Senile Dementia: A Psychobiographical Approach. *Free Associations*, 19, 60–76.

Kitwood, T. (1990b). Explaining Senile Dementia: The Limits of Neuropsychological Research. *Free Associations*, 10.

Kitwood, T. (1990). Psychotherapy and Dementia. *British Psychological Society, Psychotherapy Section Newsletter*, 8 June.

Kitwood, T. (1997). *Dementia Reconsidered: The Person Comes First*. Open University Press.

Kitwood, T. and Bredin, K. (1994). *Evaluating Dementia Care: The Dementia Care Mapping Method*. Bradford University Dementia Group.

Lewis, R. (1998). The Impact of Marital Relationship on the Experience of Caring for an Elderly Spouse with Dementia. *Ageing and Society*, 18, 209–231.

Lyman, K. (1989). Bringing the Social Back in: A Critique of the Biomedicalization of Dementia. *The Gerontologist*, 29(5).

Mackenzie-Smith, S. (1992). A Psychoanalytical Observational Study of the Elderly. *Free Associations*, 3, 355–389.

McEwan, I. (2005). *Saturday*. Jonathan Cape.

McGlynn, S. M. and Schacter, D. L. (1989). Unawareness of Deficits in Neuropsychological Syndromes. *Journal of Clinical and Experimental Neuropsychology*, 11, 143–205.

Menzies, I. (1988 [1973]). Action Research in a Long-Stay Hospital. In I. Menzies-Lyth (ed.), *Containing Anxiety in Institutions: Selected Essays, vol. 1*. Free Association Books.

Miessen, B. (1993). Alzheimer's Disease, the Phenomenon of Parent Fixation and Bowlby's Attachment Theory. *International Journal of Geriatric Psychiatry*, 8(2), 147–153.

Morris, L. W., Morris, R. G., and Britton, P. G. (1988a). The Relationship between Marital Intimacy, Perceived Strain and Depression in Spouse Caregivers of Dementia Sufferers. *British Journal of Medical Psychology*, 61, 231–236.

Morris, L. W., Morris, R. G., and Britton, P. G. (1988b). Factors Affecting the Emotional Wellbeing of the Caregivers of Dementia Sufferers. *British Journal of Psychiatry*, 153, 147–156.

Murray, H. A. (1943). *Thematic Apperception Test Manual*. Harvard University Press.

National Institute for Clinical Excellence. (2004). *Scope Guidelines for Treatment and Care of People with Dementia*. Department of Health.

Obholzer, A. (2000). Foreword. In R. D. Hinshelwood and W. Skogstad (eds), *Observing Organisations: Anxiety, Defence and Culture in Health Care*. Routledge.

Phinney, A. (2002). Fluctuating Awareness and the Breakdown of the Illness Narrative in Dementia. *Dementia*, 1, 329–344.

Post, S. (1995). *The Moral Challenge of Alzheimer's Disease*. Johns Hopkins University Press.

Pratt, R. and Wilkinson, H. (2003). A Psychosocial Model of Understanding the Experience of Receiving a Diagnosis of Dementia. *Dementia*, 2, 181–199.

Robertson, J. and Robertson, J. (1967–1971). *Film Series: Young Children in Brief Separation*. New York University Film Library.

Schmid, A. H. (1990). Dementia, Related Disorders and Old Age: Psychodynamic Factors in Diagnosis and Treatment. *American Journal of Psychoanalysis*, 50, 253–262.

Seltzer, B., Vasterling J., Yoder J., and Thompson K. A. (1997). Awareness of Deficit in Alzheimer's Disease: Relation to Caregiver Burden. *The Gerontologist*, 37, 20–24.

Stern, J. M. and Lovestone, S. (2000). Therapy with the Elderly: Introducing Psychotherapy to the Multi-disciplinary Team. *International Journal of Geriatric Psychiatry*, 15, 500–505.

Terry, P. (1997). *Counselling the Elderly and their Carers*. Macmillan Press.

Waddell, M. (2000). Only Connect: Developmental Issues from Early to Late Life. *Psychoanalytic Psychotherapy*, 14(3), 239–252.

Weiner, M. B. (1988). Tuning In, Tuning Out: Clinical Observations of Interactions between Patients with Alzheimer's Disease and Others. In R. Mayeaux *et al.* (eds), *Alzheimer's Disease and Related Disorders*. Charles C. Thomas.

Woods, P. and Ashley, J. (1995). Simulated Presence Therapy: Using Selected Memories to Manage Problem Behaviours in Alzheimer's Disease Patients. *Geriatric Nursing*, 16, 9–14.

Wright, L. K. (1991). The impact of Alzheimer's Disease on the Marital Relationship. *The Gerontologist*, 31, 224–326.

Wright, L. K. (1994). Alzheimer's Disease Afflicted Spouses Who Remain at Home: Can Human Dialectics Explain the Findings? *Social Sciences and Medicine*, 38(8), 1037–1046.

Chapter 5

The Fragile Thread of Connection
Living as a Couple with Dementia

> How could the complexities of being, the mechanics of our anatomy, the intelligence of our biology... the thoughts and questions and yearnings and hopes and hunger and desire and the thousand and one contradictions that inhabit us at any given moment – ever have an ending that could be marked by a date on a calendar? ... My father is both dead and alive ... He is in the past, present and future.
>
> – Hisham Matar, *The Return*

Introduction: The Ubiquity of Loss

For all of us, living with dementia or not, loss is at the centre of our experience. Discovered in those everyday moments of change and transition, in the return to school or work after a holiday, in the coming to an end of an intense experience, and inescapable in the pain and long-term aftershocks of the death of someone close. It is the knowledge of our limited time, of the inevitability, one day, of the loss of those at the centre of our emotional lives which shadows everything; each separation, each change or development in our lives gains part of its shape, the outer edge of its definition, by the finitude it reveals to us. Even if we choose not to apprehend it, or can do so only partially, lest it spoil the life that is there, this is the contour of our experience. Not just the ultimate horizon-line of the end of life, but the current lived shape of experience, determined by loss and by the prospect of loss. How do we manage this? Most obviously, by denial, by refusal to believe it can be true. For others maybe, but not for us, or those we love. Yet even if we try to hold onto this notion, it cannot last. Eventually, sooner or later, the limits that give life its shape confront us inescapably.

But, in a sense, loss is not 'over' – in death even, not a definitive full-stop; the presence of the person who is lost continues with you, in the interior of your living being, and in your experience of the world, as it goes on. Writers on dementia have talked about 'anticipatory grief' (Garner 1997); perhaps an aspect of experience which this illuminates is the loss that is current

DOI: 10.4324/9781032636498-5

alongside the presence of the person who is being lost in dementia, and the new relationship which has to be negotiated, even as the trajectory of change is towards increasing incapacity, and death. Dementia brings a physical and emotional confrontation with a progressively changing person; who is the same, yet the person as they were is being diminished in their capacity and posing challenges and demands that are new and increasing as time goes on. At the same time as facing loss there is the need to adapt to these new challenges; entailing mourning as well as adjustment to the person as they are now, in their changed and changing state. Despite the profound challenges of this situation, I have often been very moved in my work with couples living with dementia at witnessing the life that can be possible, adjustments, adaptations and connections between people that can be maintained and developed in new ways. Being with someone with dementia encompasses the sense of the person as they were in the past, which is part of who they continue to be; the present tense of how they are now and the shadow of the future – how they will be as the dementia progressively takes hold. These different, overlapping dimensions of time and identity are composite and are part of the emotional encounter with the family member or friend who is living with dementia.

Something like one in five people over 80 develop dementia and the way in which this is experienced will be as different in breadth and scope as the individual differences of the people inhabiting the illness. There is no 'account' of *the* experience of dementia (and of course there are a number of different types of dementia). But to respect the vastness of the range of such experience by a retreat into nomothetic data, into distanced and objective description, is to take away humanity from the account of the disease. And illness is illness – its objective fact and character render it an 'entity' with its own recognisable shape, which means that all who experience it also share something in common. As I shall discuss, personal relationships are of crucial importance in dementia and are profoundly challenged by the illness. In this chapter I shall explore the emotional challenges facing couples, drawing on research and clinical thinking to look at what may help to sustain relationships and support the resilience of people who are living together with dementia.

Attachment in Old Age and Dementia

First, to look at some background, what does research into the psychological experience of dementia have to tell us? Perhaps the most important concept, which has gathered increasing interest in recent years, is that of 'attachment' – which is generally associated with early, not late, life. However, as adults we do not outgrow our need for security, and attachment encompasses the whole lifespan and is particularly relevant in dementia. Attachment relationships are thought to function as a protective resource in later life

(Magai and Passman 1997; Sloggett et al. 2007) and attachment theory is important in understanding the experience of people with dementia. The process of dementia can be characterised by experiences of loss and separation from attachment figures (or the fear of this) and feelings of insecurity, as unwilling separation and disruption of attachment bonds can be a common part of the experience (Browne and Shlosberg 2006).

Looking at the impact of dementia upon the 'attachment system' of individuals with the illness, Miesen (1993) reports a high incidence of 'attachment seeking' behaviour in people with dementia, including those in later stage dementia. Other researchers have also found that 'attachment seeking' behaviour was evident in people with dementia across the range of the illness, including those with greater cognitive impairment (Browne and Shlosberg 2005). As Van Assche et al. (2013) point out, there is a convergence of evidence from studies in this field that insecure attachment is related to higher levels of BPSD (Behavioural and Psychiatric Symptoms in Dementia) and in caregivers is associated with higher levels of caregiving burden, negative appraisals of the situation and less satisfaction with perceived support, as well as higher levels of depression and anxiety. By contrast, secure attachment appears to make it easier to achieve a more accepting state of mind in relation to the losses and changes associated with dementia, and to sustain the capacity for emotional contact with the partner with dementia (Ingebretsen and Solem 2021).

Developmental Research

Given the importance of attachment in dementia, what does research have to tell us about what may help with anxieties and insecurities linked to this? Van Assche et al. (2013) point out the need to link the study of attachment in dementia with the extensive research on attachment at the other end of the lifespan and, as I shall discuss, the learning from developmental research has implications for our thinking about how to respond to the attachment needs of people with dementia. In order to explore this, we need to begin with the earliest attachment relationships we form, looking at research which helps us to understand how relationships in early life are established securely and what relevance this may have to thinking about dementia.

The fundamental message of developmental research in attachment is the importance for the infant of contact with the caregiver's mind, and of experiencing the caregiver's 'mind-mindedness', which are crucial for cognitive and emotional development and for establishing secure attachment. Ainsworth et al. (1978) demonstrate that parental sensitivity and responsiveness to infant affect is a key determinant of secure attachment; the infant needs to encounter a mind, a mindfulness of its own internal state in its primary care givers: 'it is not gratification of need that is at the heart of bonding, rather, it is the caregiver's capacity to create in her mind the infant's mental state' (Fonagy, Steele, Moran, Steele, and Higgitt 1993). This is not only at the heart of secure attachment, but also is the key to the infant's healthy emotional and cognitive development. Indeed, developmental researchers, such as Tronick (2004) have shown that when the infant's caregiver does not respond to their attempts to engage them, the coherence and complexity of their self-representation is disrupted and they move closer to states of both emotional and cognitive disorganisation, turning away and withdrawal (see also Fonagy and Target 2007; Beebe and Lachman 2015). This description of the infant's reaction to the disengagement of its object is reminiscent of observational work in dementia care settings, where the 'warehousing' of patients who, left for long periods without personal interaction, show a similar picture of disengagement and withdrawal (Davenhill et al. 2003).

Attachment needs are activated by dementia, with progressive cognitive impairment likely to cause both cognitive and emotional dis-integration in the context of the loss of opportunity for shared understanding and 'inter-subjectivity' Partners of people with dementia often express the impact of the loss of emotional contact and reciprocal communication within the couple, and one researcher writes, 'the feeling of the loss of the partner is associated with the loss of sharing or interaction with the partner. Some carers expressed this loss of communication as being 'as if only I knew what he/she was thinking' (Bull 1998; see also Lewis 1998; Murray, Schneider, Banerjee, and Mann 1999). The evidence from developmental research of the importance of mutuality and 'inter-subjectivity' (Fonagy and Target 2007) for security of attachment may therefore have particular implications for people with dementia, whose attachment relationships are changing as anchorage in their familiar relational and social world is progressively under threat. Transposing this evidence from attachment research of the importance of the 'joining of minds' may have important implications for the relationship between the person with dementia and their partner, indicating how vital may be the carer partner's sensitivity or 'going on thinking' about the experience of the partner with dementia.

Linking Developmental Research with Psychoanalytic Models: 'Containment'

The research finding of the importance of the caregiver's responsiveness to the infant's mental state brings us close to a core concept in psychoanalysis, that of 'containment'. Both research in infant development as well as psychoanalytic studies show us that, in good enough circumstances, our closest relationships can be the crucible of emotional growth throughout our lives. At the different developmental stages that we traverse, what is crucial is the sense of connection that comes from emotional contact with another mind that can understand and give words to our experience; or find other articulations or connections that go beyond words. As we are growing and developing as infants, we need this connection with our mother or primary attachment figures to enable our minds to grow, and throughout our lives, such emotional contact with others allows us to experience our thoughts and feelings in ways that enhance our sense of understanding, as of feeling understood. This is expressed in the concept of 'containment', which is a word that is often used in health and social care settings, but what does it mean in psychoanalytic terms? According to its originator, Bion (1962), if the mother is able to take in and think about her baby's distress, it can become 'detoxified' and the baby may be able to take back in its feelings in a more manageable form. As it does so, over time, the range of feelings that the infant can encompass in its own mental apparatus, expands – and the capacity of the caregiver to take in, think about and give meaning to experience is internalised. As I shall discuss, this model of 'container-contained', with its roots in the earliest relations of infancy can be extended to other relationships throughout the lifespan. 'Containment' is closely linked to another concept, that of 'projective identification'. This is a process that is also described in terms of early development, but again, which persists throughout life, whereby feelings, particularly frightening and disturbing ones, which the infant cannot express verbally, are got rid of by projecting them out into others, who then become identified with what has been projected into them. The recipient of these projections, such as the mother, then, if she is open to them, in her 'reverie', has the chance to experience the baby's feelings, and so such 'projection' is both a communication about, as well as a defence against, feelings and experiences which are felt to be unmanageable.

From a psychoanalytic perspective, the common element in the emotional task facing family and other carers of people with dementia may be the importance of providing containment. In dementia, increasingly the carer partner becomes the witness, whose mind can register and think about what is happening to the person with dementia whose own capacities are progressively diminished.

> If the caregiver can offer a mentally receptive state of mind, conscious or unconscious, the communication can be received, modified if it is one of pain and rage, appreciated if one of love and pleasure, and recommunicated ... The caregiver's mind functions as a container for, and a sorter of, the projected emotional fragments, which, as a consequence, become the 'contained'.
>
> (Waddell 2007)

This highlights the importance of trying to understand the communications of individuals with dementia, as often conveyed through projective processes. Windows of clarity, of a briefly more integrated state may be opened for the person with dementia by trying to understand them, thereby making emotional contact and finding some way – either in words or action –of conveying that understanding. Waddell (2007), drawing on the disquisition on the Seven Ages of Man from 'As You Like It', by Shakespeare, points out that, even in the profound losses of dementia, there might be moments of recovery, of 'ripening' amid the 'rotting'. To what extent, as the pressure of the illness increases and capacities are lost, more persecuted states of mind may begin to dominate is unclear – but the clinical case study evidence is that, to some degree at least, this depends on how much containment can be offered by the partner without dementia.

Understanding and the Importance of Emotional Contact in Dementia

> How well others understand you and you them, makes more difference to your life than what you own.
> – Theodore Zeldin, *The Hidden Pleasures of Life*

While there may be evidence of the importance of emotional contact, of the act of seeking to understand in dementia, the situation is different from that of infancy where there is development of mind and growth towards separation and greater somatic and psychic integrity. Needless to say, the situation of dementia reverses this developmental trajectory; what is ahead is increasing dependency, loss of autonomy and mental functioning and ultimately, death. Consequently, the context for emotional contact and awareness of the mind of self and other is different; now it is loss that is at the heart of things, not developmental gains and pleasure at this, as is the prospect in infancy. While recovered understanding and moments of mutuality and emotional contact may be of crucial importance in dementia, they can be difficult to achieve, facing the individual – both person with dementia and their partner – with considerable psychic challenges. Most particularly, the capacity to bear and contain feelings such as loss, anger and – for the carer partner in particular – frustration and guilt, may be necessary to support engagement with the emotional realities of the situation; and such feelings can themselves be brought to life and amplified by emotional contact in the relationship between the partners living with dementia. This raises the question of what supports may be needed to help the couple facing such a challenging emotional situation at this stage of life, which does not contain the hope for the future which sustains the 'nursing couple' of mother and infant. For both partners in couples living with dementia, containment is crucial to support continued thinking and engagement with experience; and to help the carer to contain the emotional needs of the person with dementia.

The challenges can be profound, both for the person with dementia and their partner and it is understandable that carers who are themselves less contained may be less able to tolerate emotional contact with the person with dementia. To provide such 'containment', partners without dementia need considerable support, respite and containment themselves. It is very difficult for any of us to take in and think about the experience of someone else, if we ourselves are not feeling understood and 'taken in' emotionally. To borrow a phrase from mother–infant psychotherapy: 'the mother whose cries are heard hears her infant's cries' (Fraiberg 1987). This is a crucial issue in working in this area: not simply to exhort the partner without dementia to think more closely about what is happening in their partner's mind, but to think with them about their own feelings in order that, once they themselves are feeling better understood, they may 'think their way' into their partner's shoes better and tolerate greater engagement with both their own and their partner's emotional experience.

Emotional Engagement with the Experience of Dementia

One woman described her husband's ability to help her with disturbing and frightening states of mind and the importance of being with someone felt to have the capacity to take in her fears, and help her with her feelings:

> I was having hallucinations – my husband was able to put my mind at ease. They were awful –but he would rescue me – bring me back ... I could hear him coming up the stairs and I wasn't afraid because I could hear it was him. If it hadn't been for him telling me that I was seeing things I would have been terrified –I have feelings or sensations or dreams that are genuinely frightening. On the whole he is the one person who can calm me down ... he is the only one who wanted to understand.

Another person living with dementia conveyed how holding onto her anchorage in herself and her sense of what she could do was easily lost in the face of the difficulties that she faced as she tried to manage ordinary activities of life. It was hard for her to keep on struggling to remember, to think, to recover what she could – and she said that thinking about it could make it worse, at times. She told me she had seen some rabbits in the park and had asked herself, what do the rabbits think and feel? What capacity do they have to reflect – to feel emotions? She asked, how is her mind now and how will it be in the future? The rabbits will probably get devoured and killed off; these are cruel losses, she said, thinking of herself being devoured by the disease which was eating away her mind. She remembered a lot but saw evidence all the time of what she was not remembering, of what had got lost. It seemed that she was trying to hold onto her connection with the world, to a state of mind where she felt there were things which could still be enjoyed. However, the difficulty with engaging in thinking and staying involved exposed her more to what she could not do, confronting her with the realities of her illness. All the time, she said, she had thoughts like 'I should have known that, reproachful thoughts'. This seemed to be the dilemma of her continued engagement and thinking, and trying to do things confronted her with what she could no longer manage – with the reality of new limits and loss of capacity. However, her experience of emotional contact with her partner and with the therapist in their joint discussions seemed also to lead to a shift in her state of mind. She went on to say, at other times – and she felt it could change quite quickly – she could feel more hopeful. 'There are things I look forward to – seeing people, family – walks …' and she said she had thought of taking up music again: 'there are things I can do to hold back the AD, not to give up', she said. 'If I could find a teacher who would take someone like me, with my difficulties – what could be recovered and held on to?'

She said that she used to work with people who had been recovering from drug addiction, helping them rehabilitate – trying to bring their minds to life, and she spoke of how important this had been to her. In our work, it seemed, she felt that there was an interest in her and her feelings and perhaps the experience of this helped her to feel her mind to be alive; for a moment in time she could hold onto the music inside herself, so to speak. What felt to be of significance in the work, was her experience of others seeking to understand her – and that it was the act of trying to understand, rather than of any special 'understanding', which enabled an atmosphere of emotional contact and meaning-making to emerge as part of a shared communicative endeavour. In encountering her experience at such close hand, I felt I was the recipient of hard-wrought communication of her continued struggle to stay emotionally engaged, despite the profoundly difficult feelings this confronted her with, in facing the depredations of dementia.

The Couple with Dementia

It has been said that the physical and psychological health of older couples is linked 'for better or for worse'. Researchers have found strong associations between depressive symptoms and 'functional limitations' (the physical inability to perform basic tasks of everyday living) between the partners in older couples: spouse's symptoms wax and wane closely with those of their partners (Hoppmann et al. 2011). Such findings show how interdependent emotionally and physically older couples are and highlight the need for a health and social care system that does not just focus on individuals in isolation.

There is now a building evidence base indicating that the quality of the couple relationship affects carers' well-being and in particular, the continued sense of connection between partners is linked to lower distress levels, lower burden and higher caregiver competence (Lewis et al. 2005). Research studies converge in their findings that dementia impacts upon the couple's relationship in terms of diminished companionship, communication, reciprocity and intimacy (Evans and Lee 2014). However, some studies have also emphasised continuities that can be maintained within the relationship and individual differences between couples in their response to dementia. Despite the losses and changes found by many studies, the qualitative literature in particular highlights case examples where feelings of belonging, reciprocity and continuity within close relationships in couples living with dementia were important (Hellstrom and Lund 2007; see Wadham et al. 2016 for a review). Forsund et al. (2014) found that couples' experiences fluctuated dynamically, with recovered moments of connectedness, reciprocity and interdependence which were reported as being invaluable for the spouses of people with dementia. These authors point out the importance of identifying, understanding and validating the shared experiences of both partners to support the sense of inter-connectedness in the couple relationship in dementia.

For couples, the experience of dementia occurs in the context of a relationship which pre-dates the dementia often by the best part of a lifetime, and the pre-morbid quality of the relationship affects how dementia is experienced (Ablitt et al. 2010). Carers who report lower relationship quality prior to the onset of dementia report greater depression, distress and emotional reactivity to the challenges of caring (Gilleard et al. 1984; Knop et al. 1998), and strain (Morris et al. 1988b). However, even if things up to now have been good enough, the couple living with dementia are losing a relationship in which they have provided containment for each other. In a relatively healthy adult relationship where projections are not too fixed, partners may be able to act as containers of difficult feelings for one another in a flexible way. In a relationship where one partner has a dementia, the burden will increasingly shift to the partner without dementia to act as container for their spouse. Carer partners, particularly men, often speak of this as a 'reversal' of how things had been before. One man said: 'It used to be me who was the one who was more shut down. Now it has switched around and she is the one who is more like I used to be ... now we are crossing over into opposite places.'

For the couple with dementia, we are not just talking about losing the person as they once were nor of a reversal of a projective system, but the person with dementia may start to project feelings in a way which is very persecuting, and this may become amplified as the disease progresses and projection replaces language. The carer partner may increasingly be needed to be the container in the relationship, but they are likely to be filled with feelings of loss, frustration – fears and anxieties – and so it may be very difficult for them to take in their partner's projections or state of mind. As I have said, offering containment for the partner without dementia is crucial, so that their capacity to be emotionally available is supported. The presence of a third containing figure, someone the carer partner is able to talk to about the reality of their feelings, can be very important.

In summary, the person without dementia may be struggling with their own feelings of loss, frustration and other feelings – and the stage is set for a difficult situation. Although every relationship is unique, we can nevertheless extrapolate some general descriptions of the dynamics of couple relationships affected by dementia:

- How things were in the past is likely to colour very profoundly the experience of the intrusion of dementia into the relationship.
- We all use projective identification all of the time – and in this model, it is also the basis of empathy, and testing out your understanding of what the other person is feeling.
- In well-functioning relationships, an important factor is the flexibility in the couple's projective system, partners 'taking projections back'/reality testing their perceptions of one another.
- Under optimal conditions, in a relationship there will be a flexible interchange of projections between the partners, for example, the looking-after role in the relationship.
- The difficulty for the couple living with dementia is that where projections may once have been more fluid, this is inevitably changed by the illness.
- Encroaching dependency and loss of capacity can carry with it fears of a state of traumatic return to earlier states of dependency.
- The person with dementia loses more and more their anchorage in the world. 'I get frightened when he goes out of the room' is a comment often made, expressing the insecurity felt by many people with dementia.
- The partner without dementia can feel tremendous pressure when faced with their partner's vulnerability and need, where the memory of the reassurance that they will be back soon is lost a few minutes later.
- As language is lost so increasingly projective processes replace verbal communication. Now increasingly the burden shifts to the carer partner to provide a containing mind.
- This can entail a very significant emotional burden for the carer partner.
- There is a need to 'contain the container' – to help the carer partner to process their experiences, so that they are able to be emotionally available to their partner with dementia.
- Dementia can, in a sense, feel infectious – and the concept of projective identification is useful as a way of understanding this; how the dementia is also a couple experience, with unconscious as well as conscious areas of experience that are held within the couple.

The following case example illustrates the value of seeking to understand the issues facing a couple living with dementia. Many themes discussed in this chapter are evident, such as the 'infectiousness' of dementia, and the significance of containment in the recovery of emotional contact and resilience. Above all, this example shows how these ideas can help guide us towards establishing a shared 'language of meaning' in working with a couple living with dementia.

Case Example: Working with a Couple Who Are Living with Dementia

Dementia lands on the dynamics of the relationship which were there before the illness, and often its impact will be felt on familiar 'fault lines'. A dilemma which couples of all ages can struggle with, is the threat of loss of individual identities in the relationship and for this couple, this longstanding difficulty had been exacerbated by the dementia. At the start of the work, they said they felt like 'Siamese twins' – as they were 'thrown back upon themselves' by the dementia. This was a claustrophobic situation which was familiar, although the dementia had robbed them of their established defences, their previous 'escape routes' – having had separate bases, often working for long periods apart. Although these old 'solutions' were lost, the familiar dynamic was re-established in their new situation of dementia– and their lack of psychic separateness which previously had been managed by physical distance and separation, now felt more claustrophobic than ever.

He was immersed in her world of dementia – he said that he wanted to live through it alongside her, but felt he was struggling to keep his head above water. He felt submerged at times, he said, and was strongly identified with her experience. He described how he was trying to keep his own mind alive, through reading – though he struggled to write or engage in his creative work. Now he felt it was as though he didn't exist anymore. His role was gone and at times he felt that she was the one who seemed more content and to be coping better – he felt anxious, cut off from people – displaced from his old roles, from himself. It seemed that for both of them there was a feeling of being displaced. He was struggling with his identity which she was also doing. He was not working on a writing project and he had lost his anchorage in his sense of creativity and purpose. He had health problems of his own, requiring treatment and he was frightened of that, he said. The old struggle, of how to manage each of their individual needs, which were felt to threaten to negate the other's, had not gone away, appearing now in a new guise, of whose health would take priority. On one occasion, they'd had a row about whose needs should prevail and he'd felt she was 'putting the knife into him'. This is perhaps an image that captures the projective identification, of how her state of mind was projected into him, and was infectious, as he put it.

Over time, in the therapeutic work, there were shifts, most notably a lessening of projective identification within the couple; as there was more containment of their feelings in the work with the therapist, he became more able to tolerate his feelings and to face the losses which confronted them. As this became more established, there was evidence of more capacity in him to recover his thinking. At one session, he commented on how, before, he had been talking of being overwhelmed and fearing that he couldn't manage things and was unable to think clearly or work in a creative way. On reflection, he said, these were feelings that one might expect her to be having, and somehow he had been having them. He thought more about this and began to recognise that while these feelings of losing his sense of identity, his capacity to work and his connection with the world, were part of his own experience, they were also perhaps feelings which were hers as well. The intensity with which he felt them gave him an understanding of what she might be going through, he thought. As he reflected more on this, he felt he had an insight into her mind, into her experience. It seemed that he wasn't so much in that state of mind now and had recovered more his sense of himself, his own mind and intellectual life – and he started writing again. It seemed that, as he felt he had more internal and external support and that he was more anchored in his own, separate mind, he was then more able to be alongside her and to engage with her, without withdrawing so much in anger or frustration.

His identification with her had maintained the lack of psychic separateness between them and perhaps functioned to avoid the experience of loss, though it had compounded the resentment and claustrophobia of the situation. As more psychic separateness emerged, they were more in touch with the emotional pain of the losses they faced. At one session, he spoke about the loss and the changes that they had to adjust to as a couple and added that it also made him think of the past – how there had been real costs of his decision to live away from her for all that time when they were younger. There had been impacts on her, on the family – losses, and time that they could not have back: 'I always thought that there would be more time, but some things are lost and that's it – they don't come back, and you don't get a second chance.'

He was faced by his guilt and by the limits of reparation that were possible at this point, now that the dementia was in process; and things could not, in reality, be 'made better' anymore. What emerged more clearly was how such guilt impoverished the emotional contact that might still be possible between them; amplifying the difficulty in facing the losses that confronted them and fuelling his defensive retreat into anger and withdrawal from her. Anxiety about his aggression, and his frustration with her, made it harder for him to be close to her; he feared that he would be damaging towards her – and this compounded the guilt he felt. As he became more able to tolerate these feelings, and to articulate them, he spoke of his wish to make it up to her, for his unavailability before; and although the clock could not be turned back, there was the sense of reparative processes beginning to emerge, of the wish to make some repair while there was still time. He began to engage with her more closely when he was with her, allowing more emotional contact between them. She seemed to recognise this: 'The other night, we were going to sleep with our fingers linked together – touching our hands, and that hasn't happened for a few weeks.'

It seemed that when he engaged with her and did things together with her, he was more painfully in touch with the losses which faced them. He said, each time he thought of something they could still do, he asked himself, would this be the last time? Would she be able to work with him, alongside him again, in the garden next spring? At the same time, he conveyed the preciousness of the moments of 'togetherness' with her, which were still possible, even as he mourned their loss:

> We are trying to find ways to manage to hold onto things we can do, not to give up, though it is very painful ... What if the link that we have now gets lost? ... I am afraid that the fragile thread of connection that we have, that we have held onto, will get lost forever ...

The toleration of these losses allowed more emotional contact between them and, over time, greater capacity to bear this enhanced their intimacy and shared involvement in everyday activities with one another. Although such contact is very important, as I have tried to show, it can be very hard to sustain, raising the question of what is an optimal 'adjustment' to the illness? What should the aim of psychological intervention be? Perhaps one answer might be in helping to support the couple so that they might be helped to avoid premature foreclosure of emotional involvement and connection with one another, which research shows to be so important, even as this becomes more difficult as capacities are lost as the dementia unfolds.

Conclusion

Historically, there has been a neglect of the experience of dementia as a focus of study that could help shape our understanding of how best to help those living with the illness, and this has only begun to change in recent times. This may be a reflection, at the group or societal level, of the difficulty in allowing close emotional contact with the experience of those living with dementia that has been explored here at the level of the couple; an example of our human tendency to withdraw from things that we would rather not know about, dementia facing us, as it does, with the prospect of the loss of capacities that we think of as fundamental to who we are, to our very personhood. This neglect matters because, if an understanding of the experiences of people with dementia and those living with them is not more at the heart of our approaches to dementia care, then we will fail to learn how best to support people with the emotional challenges they face. Significant change in the quality of our services will only be achieved if the experiences of people living with dementia can be brought out of obscurity into the open; if the 'private lives' of these more intimate aspects of experience can be put at the centre of our thinking about dementia, allowing us to develop greater understanding of the emotional supports that are needed to help sustain relationships and to hold people in their familiar relational context, supporting the resilience of couples and families living with the illness.

To this end, we need to draw on what we know from research and clinical practice about the importance of emotional contact and containment in mitigating attachment insecurity and supporting the person with dementia's anchorage in the world of meaning and human relationships. From the beginning of our lives, we need to be understood, to link with others whose capacity to take us in and understand our emotional states enables us to develop emotionally, and to feel secure. While this is crucial at our beginning, it continues to be true throughout our lives and becomes truer again as we move towards our end. The presence of another, understanding mind is vital as mind is lost in dementia. In developing this idea, this chapter has discussed the evidence of attachment research across the lifespan, linking this to the psychoanalytic concept of containment in dementia care and the importance of this for supporting the emotional resources of couples and families and enabling them to live more emotionally satisfying lives together, with dementia.

References

Ablitt, A., Jones, G. V., Muers, J. (2010). Living with Dementia: A Systematic Review of the Influence of Relationship Factors. *Aging and Mental Health*, 13(4), 497–511. (doi:10.1080/13607860902774436)

Ainsworth, M. (1978). *Patterns of Attachment: A Psychological Study of the Strange Situation*. Lawrence Erlbaum Associates.

Balfour, A., Morgan, M., and Vincent, C. (2012). *How Couple Relationships Shape Our World: Clinical Practice, Research and Policy Perspectives*. Karnac.

Beebe, B. and Lachman, F. M. (2015). The Expanding World of Edward Tronick. *Psychoanalytic Enquiry*, 35(4), 328–366.

Bion, W. R. (1962). *Learning from Experience*. Heinemann.

Browne, C. J., and Shlosberg, E. (2005). Attachment Behaviours and Parent Fixation in People with Dementia: The Role of Cognitive Functioning and Pre-morbid Attachment Style. *Aging and Mental Health*, 9(2), 153–161.

Browne, C. J., and Shlosberg, E. (2006). Attachment Theory, Ageing and Dementia: A Review of the Literature. *Aging and Mental Health*, 10(2), 134–142.

Bull, M. A. (1998). Losses in Families Affected by Dementia: Coping Strategies and Service Issues. *Journal of Family Studies*, 4, 187–199.

Davenhill, R., Balfour, A., Rustin, M., Blanchard, M., and Tress, K. (2003). Looking into Later-Life: Psychodynamic Observation and Old Age. *Psychoanalytic Psychotherapy*, 17(3), 254–266.

Evans, D., and Lee, E., (2014). Impact of Dementia on Marriage: A Qualitative Systematic Review. *Dementia* 13, 330–349.

Fonagy, P., and Target, M. (2007). Playing with Reality. IV. A Theory of External Reality Rooted in Intersubjectivity. *International Journal of Psychoanalysis*, 88, 917–937.

Fonagy, P., Steele, M., Moran, G., Steele, H., and Higgitt, A. (1993). Measuring the Ghost in the Nursery: An Empirical Study of the Relation between Parents' Mental Representations of Childhood Experiences and Their Infants' Security of Attachment. *Journal of the American Psychoanalytic Association*, 41, 957–989.

Forsund, L. H., Skovdhl, K., Kiik, R., and Ytrehus, S. (2014). The Loss of a Shared Lifetime: A Qualitative Study Exploring Spouses' Experiences of Losing Couplehood with their Partner with Dementia Living in Institutional Care. *Journal of Clinical Nursing*, 24, 121–130.

Fraiberg, S. (1987). Ghosts in the Nursery. In L. Fraiberg (ed.), *Selected Writings of Selma Fraiberg*. Ohio State University Press.

Garner, J. (1997). Dementia: An Intimate Death. *British Journal of Medical Psychology*, 70(2), 177–184.

Gilleard, C. J., Belford, H., Gilleard, E., Whittick, J. E., and Gledhill, K. (1984). Emotional Distress amongst the Supporters of the Elderly Mental Infirm. *British Journal of Psychiatry*, 145, 172–177.

Hellstrom, I. and Lund, U. (2007). Sustaining 'Couplehood': Spouses' Strategies for Living Positively with Dementia. *Dementia*, 6, 383–409.

Hoppmann, C., Gerstorf, D., and Hibbert, A. 2011. Spousal Associations Between Functional Limitation and Depressive Symptom Trajectories: Longitudinal Findings from the Study of Asset and Health Dynamics Among the Oldest Old (AHEAD). *Health Psychology*, 30(2), 153–162.

Ingebretsen, R., and Solem, P. E. (2021). Attachment, Loss and Coping in Caring for a Dementing Spouse. In B. M. L. Miesen and G. M. M. Jones (eds), *Care-Giving in Dementia*. Routledge.

Knop, D. S., Bergman-Evans, B., and McCabe, B. W. (1998). In Sickness and in Health: An Exploration of the Perceived Quality of the Marital Relationship, Coping and Depression in Caregivers of Spouses with Alzheimer's Disease. *Journal of Psychosocial Nursing*, 36, 16–21.

Lewis, R. D. H. (1998). The Impact of the Marital Relationship on the Experience of Caring for an Elderly Spouse with Dementia. *Ageing and Society*, 18(2), 209–231.

Lewis, M. L., Hepburn, K., Narayan, S., and Kirk, L. N. (2005). Relationship Matters in Dementia Caregiving. *American Journal of Alzheimer's Disease and Other Dementias*, 20(6), 341–347.

Magai, C., and Passman, V. (1997). The Interpersonal Basis of Emotional Behavior and Emotion Regulation in Adulthood. *Annual Review of Gerontology and Geriatrics*, 17, 104–137.

Matar, H. (2016). *The Return: Fathers, Sons and the Land in Between*. Viking.

Miesen, B. (1993). Alzheimer's Disease, the Phenomenon of Parent Fixation and Bowlby's Attachment Theory. *International Journal of Geriatric Psychiatry*, 8(2), 147–153.

Morgan, M. (2016). An Object Relations Approach to the Couple Relationship: Past, Present and Future. *Couple and Family Psychoanalysis*, 6(2), 194–205.

Morris, L. W., Morris, R. G., and Britton, P. G. (1988a). The Relationship between Marital Intimacy, Perceived Strain and Depression in Spouse Caregivers of Dementia Sufferers. *British Journal of Medical Psychology*, 61, 231–236.

Morris, L. W., Morris, R. G. and Britton, P. G. (1988b). Factors Affecting the Emotional Wellbeing of the Caregivers of Dementia Sufferers. *British Journal of Psychiatry*, 153, 147–156.

Murray, J., Schneider, J., Banerjee, S., and Mann, A. (1999). EUROCARE: A Cross-National Study of Co-resident Spouse Carers for People with Alzheimer's Disease. II. A Qualitative Analysis of the Experience of Caregiving. *International Journal of Geriatric Psychiatry*, 14(8), 662–667.

Sloggett, A., Young, H., and Grundy, E. (2007). The Association of Cancer Survival with Four Socioeconomic Indicators: A Longitudinal Study of the Older Population of England and Wales 1981–2000. *BMC Cancer*, 7, 20.

Tronick, E. (2004). Why Is Connection with Others so Critical? The Formation of Dyadic States of Consciousness and the Expansion of Individuals' States of Consciousness: Coherence Governed Selection and the Co-creation of Meaning Out of Messy Meaning Making. In J. Nadel and D. Muir (eds), *Emotional Development*. Oxford University Press.

Van Assche, L. V., Luyten, P., Bruffaerts, R., Perssons, P., van de Ven, L., and Vandenbulcke, M. (2013). Attachment in Old Age: Theoretical Assumptions, Empirical Findings and Implications for Clinical Practice. *Clinical Psychology Review*, 33, 67–81.

Waddell, M. (2007) Only Connect: The Links Between Early and Later Life. In R. Davenhill (ed.), *Looking into Later Life: A Psychoanalytic Approach to Depression and Dementia in Old Age*. Karnac.

Wadham, O., Simpson, J., Rust, J., and Murray, C. (2016). Couples' Shared Experiences of Dementia: A Meta-synthesis of the Impact upon Relationships and Couplehood. *Aging and Mental Health*, 20(5), 463–473.

Wright, L. (1991). The Impact of Alzheimer's Disease on the Marital Relationship. *The Gerontologist*, 31, 224–326.

Wright, L. (1994) Alzheimer's Disease Afflicted Spouses Who Remain at Home: Can Human Dialectics Explain the Findings? *Social Sciences and Medicine*, 3(8), 1037–1046.

Zeldin, T. (2015). *The Hidden Pleasures of Life: A New Way of Remembering the Past and Imagining the Future*. Hachette.

Chapter 6

Working Psychotherapeutically with Couples Who Are Living with Dementia

This chapter discusses an approach to working with couples where one partner has a dementia, called 'Living Together with Dementia' (LTwD). This draws upon video-based methods that have been used with parents and children as well as from psychoanalytic couple psychotherapy, to develop an intervention to assist emotional contact, communication and understanding in couples living with dementia. Our approach includes the person with dementia and their partner, focusing upon the relationship between them and using shared involvement in everyday activities as a basis for enhancing emotional contact. Evidence is reviewed of the need for such an approach, which aims to foster the resilience of the couple's relationship and strengthen their capacity to manage the emotional challenges of the situation. The importance of services holding a relational view in their delivery, and the economic and humanitarian consequences of a neglect of this in dementia care settings, are also discussed.

More than 30 years ago, when I was beginning my career as a clinical psychologist, I had the task of giving an elderly man a diagnosis of dementia. I had nothing to offer him and his wife, except an information leaflet and then I watched them through the window, going out of the hospital grounds, supporting each other as they walked away in the rain. I have never forgotten this image. It is now three decades later, and not much has changed. Although there are more psychosocial interventions for early-stage dementia, availability is inconsistent and limited. And few of the interventions that are available recognise dementia as an illness that affects not only individuals but also relationships. Yet around the world, most people who have dementia are looked after at home by their spouse or partner, and only about thirty per cent ever go into residential care (Pozzebon et al. 2016). Researchers (McGovern 2011) suggest the need to recontextualise the experience of dementia as an illness affecting relationships rather than individuals. This is a conceptual shift that supports the development of services and policies geared towards encouraging togetherness rather than separateness – and focusing on family systems rather than individuals.

Dementia is an umbrella term for a range of progressive conditions that affect the brain. Each type of dementia prevents a person's brain cells

DOI: 10.4324/9781032636498-6

(neurones) from working properly in specific areas, affecting their ability to remember, think and speak. There are more than 200 subtypes of dementia, according to Dementia UK. The most common are Alzheimer's disease, vascular dementia, Lewy body dementia, frontotemporal dementia and mixed dementia (Dementia UK 2023). In 2019, there were an estimated 748,000 older people living with dementia in England; this number is predicted to grow to 1.35 million by 2040 (LSE 2019). The LSE (2019) also estimated the total cost of dementia in England in 2019 was £29.5 billion – and it is expected to increase to £80.4 billion by 2040. Studies show that providing carers with emotional support earlier on delays subsequent admission to residential care of the person with dementia by an average of 500 days (Brodaty et al. 1997). Indeed, research has found that low levels of positive interaction in the marriages of people with dementia predict the move to residential care and the death of the spouse with dementia two years later (Wright 1991, 1994). Closer relationships between the carer and the person with dementia are associated with slower decline in Alzheimer's disease, and this effect is highest for couple relationships (Norton et al. 2009).

Many people are looked after by their partners at home, at least in the early stages of dementia. Efforts in health and social policy are also, at present, directed towards encouraging home treatment. Carers of people with dementia save the taxpayer £5 billion a year, according to a report to a Public Accounts Committee. The committee was also told that carers do not get the support they need and many feel abandoned after the diagnosis. The burden of cost on the carer is more than economic, with the role placing 'a mental and physical burden ... leading to poorer outcomes and health inequalities' (Nigel Hawkes, *The Times*, 24 January 2008). Partners of people with dementia are usually the carers who experience the heaviest burden (Cantor 1983) often suffering from stress and burnout. At worst, insecure attachment in people with dementia, as well as their caregivers, is related to higher levels of behavioural and psychological symptoms in dementia (Van Assche et al. 2013). Research also shows that dementia affects spousal relationships by causing decline in communication, opportunities for shared activities and happiness.

As discussed in the previous chapter, while dementia impacts upon the couple's relationship in terms of diminished companionship, communication, and intimacy (Evans and Lee 2014), some studies have emphasised what might also be held onto, giving examples where feelings of belonging and reciprocity within close relationships in couples living with dementia were sometimes possible to maintain (Hellstrom and Lund 2007; Wadham et al. 2016). Research has also shown that, if couples can find ways of maintaining continuities in their lives together and find new ways of relating to one another in the context of dementia, this may help them to adapt to the challenges of the illness (McGovern 2011). Indeed, there is now strong evidence which shows the importance of a sense of inter-connectedness in the couple relationship in dementia and the value of understanding and validating the shared experiences of both partners to support this. There is a profound need for such a 'relationship focused' approach (McGovern 2011; Henderson and Forbat 2002) which offers more hope than focusing exclusively on cognitive decline. This is of crucial importance given the intense distress, despair and hopelessness that such couples can face (Wadham et al. 2016, p. 471).

The Living Together with Dementia Intervention

'Living Together with Dementia' (LTwD) is a structured approach to working with couples where one partner has a dementia, which draws upon psychoanalytic thinking and therapeutic methods developed in working with parents and children which emphasise observation and use video as part of their focus. These include Parent–Infant Psychotherapy (Baradon et al. 2005), Video Interaction Guidance (Kennedy, Landor, and Todd 2011), and the Relationship Development Intervention (Gutstein 2005), an approach to working with children with autism and their parents, as well as techniques from couple psychotherapy. The LTwD intervention uses everyday domestic activities as opportunities for shared endeavour and involvement for the couple. The focus is upon the emotional meaning and potential of these everyday activities to support inter-dependency between the partners (what Uchino et al. 1994 called 'cohesion'), and to address some of the relational impacts which are identified by dementia research as linked to negative outcomes for both partners. Our aim is to support couples as much as possible to maintain, or recover, the protective aspects of their relationship, which research indicates are to do with emotional contact and understanding, shared activity and involvement as well as the overall quality of their relationship. Our intention is to hold the couple, for longer in a position where they are in emotional contact with one another and to give them tools which help to counteract the pressure towards withdrawal between the partners, which is so often associated with dementia.

My interest in the application of psychoanalytic thinking in this area began when working in hospital settings where there was little place for thinking about the meaning of the behaviour and communications of people with dementia. This experience highlighted the relevance of a psychoanalytic approach which seeks to understand more extreme and primitive anxieties and offers a model for understanding that our need for our feelings to be taken in and understood throughout our lives, is of central importance for our development and for the security of our attachments to others. The central point I am making in this chapter is of the relevance of a psychoanalytic emphasis on the value of understanding and containing feelings in dementia, where it is the capacity to think and to understand which is being lost – and just how difficult this can be – whether for formal care staff or for partners in relationships of many years' standing. They themselves need support and containment of their feelings to be better able to do this for their partners as the illness progresses. When people are facing intense anxieties, confusion or loss of meaning, there is a tremendous need for them to encounter a mind, or a mindful environment, and too often there can be what Davenhill (2007) has termed a 'malignant mirroring' – a premature foreclosure of meaning in the environment of care giving. In dementia care, there is often an inverse relationship between how much support and containment staff receive, and how close to the front line of service delivery they are, those most in need often receiving least. This is corrosive to the people with dementia themselves, to staff and to the couple relationship and can be one of the bleakest aspects of dementia.

I will give an outline of the process of the intervention, drawing on case examples to describe some of the important themes that have emerged in our work.

Containment

In the post-diagnosis phase, the initial emphasis of assessment and intervention is on engaging the couple, exploring their experiences, and focusing on the containment of their feelings. Couples may have to manage considerable anxiety, and dementia may carry the threat of being abandoned to a state of utter helplessness, which may also at an unconscious level evoke fears of a traumatic return to earlier states of dependency.

One important notion to keep in mind is the process of the dementia, and that the needs of the couple will change as it goes on. As Sinason points out:

> The difference between someone at the start of Alzheimer's Disease and someone who is near the end is as large as someone who is normal and someone who is profoundly handicapped. The total continuum is experienced in the mind and heart of a single being.
>
> (Sinason 1992, p. 89)

If we think of the original (Bion 1962) model of containment, what is entailed is the taking in, and processing of experience (in the original developmental model, the mother is doing this for the infant) and conveying that understanding back so that unmanageable experience is rendered more digestible, and can be taken in, in a modified form. As I described in previous chapters, Waddell (2007) points out how windows of clarity of a briefly more integrated state may be opened for the person with dementia when emotional contact is made through finding some way, in words or action, of conveying that understanding to them.

It is important for couples facing the diagnosis of dementia that such a containing mind is available, when a mind is being lost, and when partners who may have contained each other, are becoming less able to do so. The partner who does not have dementia may find it hard to bear feelings such as anger and disappointment, particularly, perhaps, at a time when their partner is more vulnerable. Research suggests that containment at this point may set the stage for what happens later on: with the finding that providing carers with emotional support earlier on delays admission to residential care later on in the illness (Brodaty et al. 1997).

Recognising the Emotional Challenge Facing the Carer Partner

It is important to recognise the tremendous challenge facing the carer, and not to gloss over this or idealise what is possible. This draws our attention to the importance of the state of mind of the carer partner and their need for support and containment. They may have all kinds of feelings towards the individual with dementia in their care, apart from compassionate ones, such as resentment or hatred. These feelings might arouse tremendous guilt or anxiety and there may be a great need for help and containment with this. And yet, approaches to interventions with carers generally do not address this more difficult area.

One person said to me: 'There are all these images everywhere of rosy carers on all the leaflets – but it's not like that ... I hate her a lot of the time and it's shit – and it's like no one can tell the truth – how shit it is, and the resentment ... What do I do with that?'

If we think about the concept of projective identification, we might recognise how difficult the task of sustaining emotional contact can be under such circumstances. Having emotional contact with fragmented experience is very difficult, and it is understandable that carers with little support may be less able to tolerate emotional contact with the person with dementia and, like front-line staff, may become overwhelmed (Hinshelwood and Skogstad 2000). This was expressed clearly by a residential care worker in the Midlands in an article in the Guardian:

> The only way someone with dementia gets one-to-one care is if they are at home and looking after someone with dementia 24 hours a day is a killer. I know many cases in which the care caused the deaths of the partners.
> (Melanie McFadyean, *The Guardian*, 20 May 2005)

People often lack a way of thinking about or making sense of such feelings, particularly of guilt and shame, and often have no one to talk to about them. This highlights the importance of the carer partner having the opportunity to speak to someone who will listen non-judgmentally, to have another take them in, emotionally. This may be a huge thing in itself: for them to be able to use the therapist in this way, as someone able to acknowledge, take in and understand feelings that they may be very ashamed of having. I have come across books which resort to exhortation to the carer partner to 'embrace' the changes associated with dementia.

We have found that an important factor for the couple is the carer partner's continuing capacity to be interested in what their partner with dementia is feeling. To this end, an important aspect of our approach is supporting them to establish and sustain this state of mind. What we find helps with this, as I have said, is if they themselves have the experience of someone trying to understand how they feel and how they see things. Once this is established, when the carer partner starts to feel 'taken in' emotionally, they may be more able to allow themselves to think about their partner's experience.

One person we saw, whose husband was in the more advanced stages of dementia, spoke of how she felt that everyone expected her to be a saint and they weren't interested in what she felt about how hard it was. 'No one's interested, they don't know what it is like', she said. Her relationship with her husband had at times been violent and in my contact with them I felt I could see how important it was to have a view of their interaction in understanding this.

For this couple, their marriage had always been difficult. Looking after him repeated, for her, a version of her experience as an only child, when her mother developed profound mental health problems after the death of her father. Then, as now, she felt left alone with a burden, with no one able to understand how difficult it was for her. In recent months, his dementia had progressed significantly, and increasingly he responded to the anxiety of not knowing what to do, moments when he was disorientated, by getting angry. For her, it was much like the angry exchanges they had had for years, and she retaliated with anger and criticism of him. This was worst at times when he was in a panic and feeling lost. I witnessed how she would tell him things that he couldn't understand or have the capacity to follow; he would respond by saying he didn't know what she was talking about, that she wasn't making any sense, and she would then get angry and critical of him. It was when she became critical or angry at the moments when he was most vulnerable that he became aggressive towards her. They showed me how quickly things could ratchet up between them. When he responded to her by saying 'You're not making sense', or 'Do it yourself then', she heard this as examples of his refusal to do things, his deliberately being difficult, and it took a lot of work for her to gradually begin to shift her perceptions of such episodes and to think about what might be happening in his mind, to put herself, to some extent, into his shoes. Crucial to this shift was the stance of listening and empathising with her feelings, so that she had the experience of someone taking her in and trying to understand how she felt and how she saw things. Once this process was established, when she started to feel 'taken in' emotionally, she began to be able to allow herself to think more about what his experience might be.

The Experience of the Dementia Diagnosis

There is a need for space to explore this, allowing for fears to be put into words by both partners, including the partner with dementia, and to meet the couple where they are emotionally. One couple gave a powerful glimpse of how traumatic the diagnosis had been. Since the diagnosis, and in the period leading up to it, Brian had been very depressed. He said to me:

> When the diagnosis was made we cried every day and then every other day – and then you kind of get on with it ... What is so difficult is the hatred that I have for what is happening ... for the people that don't have this ... the hatred that I feel in here [points to his head] ... I'm fucking angry ... the hatred ... it is so hard to have that inside you [then he became very distressed]. I want understanding, but don't feel I get it ... I can't manage the hatred and the rage. There was a painful period leading up to the diagnosis – first the doctors thought it was depression and then pseudo dementia and then when the diagnosis came, it was a relief ... but the diagnosis is a terrible diagnosis – I feel normal and then it comes back in, I am reminded of it.

At an outpatient appointment he had encountered someone in the more advanced stages of dementia: 'Who was all hunched over ... a horrible picture ... Will I be like that? What happens? Do you stop recognising people? How will it be? These are the kinds of thoughts I have.' His wife added, 'It is difficult for us to think about things like this ... painful for me too.'

Under such circumstances, having a mind available to help the couple to think, process or understand their feelings, as much as they can, is crucial. Without it, partners may withdraw more from one another and there is greater danger that there will be the acting out of anger or frustration or other feelings and anxieties.

The Therapist's Role at Assessment

If we take seriously the trauma of the diagnosis for both partners, we need to recognise the importance of meeting them where they are emotionally and of offering a receptive state of mind to take in their experience. Again, and again, people spoke of feeling 'bombarded' by well-meaning staff who visited them. As one person said:

> These people coming and going, with their leaflets, their forms to fill in, saying I should apply for this or that. We don't know who they are or where they are coming from half the time ... traipsing through here. They phone up and say it's so and so calling, and I don't know them and every time it's a different person. I got really cross with someone who

came yesterday. Hopefully I have stopped it for now. We need one person who we can build a relationship with. We just don't want any more information, leaflets or forms – it's traumatic.

While the role of giving information is, of course, very important, there might be a pressure to act, to want to give something concretely like a leaflet or information when staff face helplessness and the limits of what can be done to make things better. This can place the couple in a position where they may have to take something they don't feel ready for, based on the staff's need to relieve their own anxiety. My experience of working with staff in frontline settings is of the tremendous challenge of being confronted by fragmented states of mind, particularly when there is little support or containment available to help them to do this.

The therapeutic task is to explore the main issues facing the couple, and one of the things we have found to be important is what happens to containment within the couple relationship. For many couples, until the illness, the partners may have been fulfilling this function for each other and this has been interfered with by the dementia. The therapist needs to ask themselves, how are the couple functioning now? What are the points of maximum pressure and what kind of support will help them; what aspects of the couple's relationship provide resilience?

A focus of the assessment is identifying the issues that feel to be important in the relationship. Although someone who is trained as a couple therapist will have a model for thinking about this, we hope that there may be a range of professionals who will be able to apply this approach in their own settings by using the manual for the intervention and with training and supervision. The aim is not to train people to become couple therapists or to make 'expert' formulations; the important thing is for the therapist to model a position of curiosity, an interest in thinking about what behaviour or feelings may mean. It is the act of showing curiosity and interest which we see as the central element, in order to model the idea that there is something to think about, that both partners' experiences are meaningful and worthy of attention.

Changes in the Couple's Relationship

As I have discussed in the previous chapter, dementia brings significant changes to the dynamics of the couple's relationship. In the relationship before dementia came into their lives, the couple's 'projective system' may have been fluid, with partners able to act as containers of difficult feelings for one another in a flexible way. However, once dementia takes hold there will be an inevitable shift, and, increasingly, pressure will fall upon the partner without dementia to act as container for their spouse. As I have described, many carer partners spoke of this as a 'reversal' of how things had been before, 'She looked after me, now I have to look after her, and I'm not good at it', was a comment we heard often. One man said: 'When we first got together, I used to be more shut off and my experience of being with her helped me change. She's always been so thoughtful ... now she shuts down.'

As dementia progresses, it may not simply be that patterns get reversed or amplified, but instead there may be a whole sea change. As the person with dementia deteriorates, not only are they unable to offer containment for their partner as they may once have done, but they may also be projecting something persecuting into them. So, it may become a very literal coming true of the situation of a loss not only being an absence, but instead an experience of living in the presence of something persecutory. The carer partner may increasingly be needed to be the container in the relationship, but they are likely to be filled with their own feelings of loss, frustration, or rage - their own fears and anxieties - and so it is very difficult for them to take in their partner's projections or state of mind. One can see that the stage is set for a potentially difficult situation. And so, offering containment for the healthy spouse is very important. The presence of a third containing figure, a therapist, or a counsellor who the carer partner can talk to about the reality of their feelings, who is not going to judge but who will listen, can be very powerful. The model of our intervention is akin to a Russian doll: the person with dementia contained by their partner, who is contained by the therapist, who themselves has the containment of supervision. The important thing is containing the container.

The importance of this is underlined by the pilot work we have done, where we have found that, as well as prior relationship quality, a protective factor for the couple is the carer partner's ability to see meaning in their partner with dementia's behaviour, even when they may be behaving in a way which is quite disturbed. Linked to this is the couple's ability to observe and think about their relationship with one another. Although the extent to which this can be shared will depend on the capacity of the person with dementia, we have seen the importance of helping the couple to notice and reflect on their engagement together, which can be captured visually in the video recordings taken during the work. I shall now discuss this in more detail.

The Use of Video

Video approaches have been found to be very powerful in work with parents and children, helping to promote change and new understanding. They have the tremendous advantage, given the nature of the cognitive deficits of dementia, of not relying on linguistic and symbolic communication. Through use of video, it is possible to work with couples with dementia across a range of stages of the illness to promote change through shifts of awareness. We work alongside the couple, engaging them in working together on carefully selected activities highlighting and supporting moments of emotional contact between the partners, and engaging the person with dementia in activities that they can still manage with the support of their partner. This involves carefully structuring the activities so that they are broken down into manageable tasks, and, depending on the capacity of the partner with dementia, helping the carer spouse to learn to function as a guide, enabling their partner to be as involved as they are able to be. The intention is to maximise the extent to which activities are shared, rather than, for example, taken over by the healthy partner. It is the process of the shared activity rather than the end goal that is important, and the extent to which mutuality and emotional engagement are maximised.

The following example illustrates how such an approach, which is at one level focused on undertaking an everyday activity together, can create the conditions for a discussion which has much deeper emotional significance for the couple.

Jack and Mavis were watching a video of their attempt to sort out the videos in a display cabinet. Soon after the video clip began, both partners laughed, and the therapist stopped the tape and asked them about this. Jack responded, saying that he thought that Mavis was 'peeved' because he wasn't sticking with the task. The therapist asked her what she thought Jack had been feeling. Mavis said that she thought he felt parts of his life were being thrown away. The therapist picked up this comment and repeated it, asking Jack if this was right, that this was how he felt. He said: 'It feels like that … yeah …' And he then talked about how he used to go to the cinema every Saturday morning as a boy. Mavis chipped in, reminding him of the name of the cinema when he struggled to recall it. He had seen all of these people – Laurel and Hardy – all the old classics, the ones on the videos …

After a few more minutes, Jack took the initiative and asked Mavis what she was feeling. She said, 'I thought you are not going to give in, no matter how I tried to help you, you were fighting me … That's what it was, a fight … a quiet fight, but still a fight.' He agreed with this and went on to describe how the mess in the cabinet was what in Yiddish they call a 'bouja'. The therapist asked what this meant. 'A big mix-up', he said. Mavis commented, 'that's what your mind is sometimes, isn't it?' Jack agreed and then there was a discussion of how what was happening was a good example of the difficulty of helping each other with the 'bouja', the difficulty and confusion of the memory loss, and it could turn into a battle. Mavis went on to say that it didn't use to be like that:

> Everything used to be organised but now we keep not being able to find things. If anything happened to Jack, I wouldn't know where to start, to sort it all out. My mind, at the moment, is quite tidy … but this morning I had such a shock. I lost my purse.

And then Mavis described how she had become very angry with him. 'I felt such an idiot myself and then I let him have it full blast – two guns … which is a shame and I do feel sorry'.

It was possible for the therapist to explore this with them – how it seemed that Mavis could try to keep her mind 'tidy', but when she lost her purse it felt as though she were becoming forgetful too, that dementia was overtaking both of them. This was frightening for her and she became angry and attacking of Jack. Mavis said: 'It is like a precipice, and I can't afford to lose my mind or my memory because I am fighting for the two of us – and that is what it boils down to, because I have no one to rely on, you know, if I go down.'

We have found the video to be a powerful tool in helping the couple to observe what is going on between them, to enable them into a state of mind in which they are able to stand back and begin to question, or become interested in, why things are happening between them in a particular way. The idea is that, if the couple can be helped to begin to think about their everyday activities as opportunities for becoming more involved before the dementia becomes too advanced, this may be protective and give strategies and understanding that can be helpful later in the illness.

The activities we video can seem mundane and every day but being able to find new meaning and new ways of thinking precisely grounded in the couple's daily living, is very important. Things can easily become very calcified between a couple: he or she is simply like that – with nothing to be thought about – but the video can allow something to be noticed and seen afresh in a way that is powerful, and which can support change and new ways of thinking.

Setting Up the Video Work with the Couple

The intervention is manualised, and there are step-by-step instructions for the therapist to follow. The essence of the approach is that we say something like this to the couple: 'We want you to work together as a team. Can you think of something that needs to be done around the house –cleaning the fridge, for example – something that feels natural?'

The approach is both structured, focusing upon techniques for enabling greater contact around the everyday activities of life, but, as I have emphasised, is also very much about trying to enable the couple to think about their feelings. It is important that time is spent with each of the partners individually so that there is the opportunity for feelings and thoughts which may be stirred up by doing these activities to be expressed and thought about, sometimes with the couple together, and sometimes separately. Here the hope is that if the partners are more contained, they will need to take less recourse to defensive withdrawal or the acting out of anger and frustration.

The therapist goes through the video interactions looking at moments of contact between the partners, as well as points of frustration or difficulty. Noticing something with the couple, however mundane, that is difficult for them to see when they are otherwise immersed in their experience can help them to step back, observe and think about themselves and their relationship.

Case Example: Ray and Barbara

Having had a couple of initial meetings with the couple, during which a video was made of their looking at photographs together together, the therapist phoned the carer spouse, Barbara, to arrange the next visit. She told the therapist that there was no point in going ahead with the next meeting, as her partner, Ray, did not really do anything – his memory loss was too bad, and he had totally withdrawn. However, she agreed to meet, and, once the therapist had shown her the video and highlighted examples of her partner's competence, she was very taken with the examples of his capacity that she was shown. The therapist also highlighted Barbara's capacity to learn from the work done so far, to move away from her familiar, memory-testing interaction with him (she had tended to question him in a rather school mistress- type manner) and, instead, to use more declarative comments. For example, on the video there were impressive instances of where, instead of testing him with questions about what he remembered, she showed him a picture and said to him 'these are old buildings that were near your parents' house'. She supplied the context and her personal memory. And then he gave an association to it and a memory of his own, and they were both in more emotional contact with one another. This was something that the therapist had been working on with her, and using the video clip she was able to show Barbara how effectively she was putting it into practice, and how much Ray was responding to her. This helped Barbara to change her mind: she re-engaged and became very interested in the process, seeing the therapy through to its end, some months later.

I have focused on the positive aspect, but it can also be important to explore more negative feelings. Another video, this time of their clearing the fridge together, captured a moment where Barbara expressed frustration. In one part of the activity things become more difficult when Ray's role was to put things back into the fridge. Watching the video, one can see her tension from the outset. The therapist was careful to show Barbara the positive interaction first and then showed her a moment of frustration: in the corner of the screen, she can be observed putting her hands to her head in a manner which suggests rage and frustration. She asked Barbara, 'What was she feeling?' The ensuing discussion was helpful and linked to mourning the man she used to have, but there was also a discussion of her ability to focus on what she did have with him and what was possible now.

She described how she was frustrated about the fridge and other things – such as his complaints about his tinnitus, and her frustration with him felt at times, to be like a terrible noise between them. But the opportunity to think about it seemed to lead to a softening between them, and evident shifts in their relationship. He was a man whom she had described as often being hidden behind a book, shut off and withdrawn, and at this point in the work he was described by her as emerging more. On one occasion, she spoke of how she had noticed that he does come out into the kitchen now and say to her, 'Is there anything I can do?', and she thought he was making a link with the work that we had been doing. He had never done this before. This seemed to help her to tolerate the difficulties and her frustrations with him. Towards the end of the therapy Ray spoke in a way that seemed linked to a restoration of greater intimacy and a sense of being more contained by her and by the therapeutic work. Here, Ray seems to be communicating something about this:

> I have moods – particularly when my tinnitus is bad. She treads softly around me – she doesn't say anything – she is quietly responsive. I am a lucky man. My memory is not so good. She helps me, she's my rock. I do fear the couple being broken ... not staying ... that it will come to that.

Concluding Thoughts

Unfortunately, Ray's fear that they might be broken up is not unfounded. While, of course, the option of residential care is an important one, the evidence is that when there is insufficient support and few options for professionals once couples or carers become distressed, then premature, or unnecessary residential placement may be the outcome (Moniz-Cook and Manthorpe 2009). I am certainly not wanting to imply that people should simply be kept at home – many of the people with whom we work refer to thoughts about how the time will come when they would need to place their partner in residential care. But this can be a very difficult decision, rife with the potential for guilt and anxiety, and here we are not just talking about the consequences of physical separation. When the person with dementia is admitted into residential care, the experience of their partner can be that it is difficult for them to have a link with them, a continued role, and this can greatly compound the emotional difficulty of the situation for both partners. Services are not, on the whole, set up to operate in terms of taking account of couple relationships. Indeed, in some cases where both partners need residential care, it has not been uncommon for them to be placed in different care homes.

A British Institute of Human Rights case study (Sceats 2008) describes the situation of Fred and Mabel, who had been married for over 65 years. Fred was unable to walk on his own and relied on Mabel to help him move around. She was blind and used her husband as her eyes. They were separated after Fred fell ill and was moved into a residential care home. Mabel asked to come with him but was told by the local authority that she did not fit the criteria. Speaking to the media, Mabel said, 'We have never been separated in all our years and for it to happen now, when we need each other so much, is so upsetting. I am lost without him: we were a partnership.' This highlights how couples can function as a unit: Fred literally leans on her, and he functions as her eyes. This captures the interdependency of couples which can be at the physical level as with this couple, but also at the emotional level, each holding functions for one another which help them to sustain an equilibrium, and under benign conditions perhaps to function better together than either partner could do alone.

This situation is akin to that of the 1950s and 1960s in children's services, when children were routinely separated from their main caregiver in hospital. Now provision is made for mother or father to stay alongside the child, and together they are seen as the 'unit of care'. The approach of the 1950s seems archaic to us, yet the recognition of attachment and dependency needs, which is a commonplace nowadays in other areas of care, is not an established part of the thinking in older people's services, where an understanding of the importance of the couple relationship is largely missing. Such dependency and attachment issues do not stop being relevant when couples get older, or face dementia. In fact, they are particularly important, as the equilibrium of earlier times is undermined by the illness, whether the couple are living together or apart. The evidence that I cited earlier is that, if these issues are not thought about, it can be costly in terms of damage to emotional wellbeing, rate of decline in dementia, hospital admission and morbidity.

So often a false dichotomy is set up, particularly in times of austerity, between the policy makers who are concerned with cost on the one hand, and the clinicians who are focused on patient wellbeing and ideals of care, on the other. But these positions might come together here, because the older couple relationship can be a tremendous resource, able to provide care that is costly to give in institutional settings. However, real support of the resilience of the couple and protection of this potential resource depends upon recognising the emotional challenges these couples face and avoiding an idealisation of what is possible. To this end, the couple relationship needs to be thought about at different levels – at the policy level and at the level of local service provision. We need our policy makers and local commissioners to act to avoid both the monetary waste that neglect of the older couple entails, but also to address the human cost of this neglect, which is most starkly illustrated in the case of the separation of couples who may have been together a lifetime, when one or other of them becomes unable any longer to be cared for at home.

I have tried to show that there is a profound need for interventions which help relationships at this end of the lifespan and for our services to become more relationship-minded, to support the humanity of the individual with dementia and those around them, so that emotional meaning can be held onto within the environment of care for as long as possible. I think we would all wish for such an environment for ourselves and those we care about. The converse position, of avoidable admission, separation from important relationships, and lack of emotional engagement with the person with dementia in many settings, is a situation that we can recognise as profoundly damaging, as one of 'society's ills' that we need to grip in order to bring change. There are signs of development in the field, and dementia is now centre stage in terms of political and media attention, after a lifetime of neglect. My hope is that new ways of working will be developed, such as I have described in this chapter, which will be part of a process of bringing more thinking and understanding to bear on an area of life that has languished largely ignored by society, for too long 'stowed out of conscience as unpopular luggage' (Auden 1968, p. 860).

References

Ablitt, A., Jones, G. V., and Muers, J. (2009). Living with Dementia: A Systematic Review of the Influence of Relationship Factors. *Aging and Mental Health*, 13(4), 497–511.

Auden, W. H. (1968). Old People's Home. In W. H. Auden, *Selected Poems*. Faber & Faber.

Baradon, T., Broughton, C., Gibbs, I., James, J., Joyce, A., and Woodhead, J. (2005). *The Practice of Psychoanalytic Parent-Infant Psychotherapy: Claiming the Baby*. Routledge.

Bion, W. R. (1962). *Learning from Experience*. Heinemann.

Brodaty, H., Gresham, M., and Luscome, G. (1997). The Prince Henry Hospital Dementia Caregivers Training Programme. *International Journal of Geriatric Psychiatry*, 12, 183–193.

Bull, M. A. (1998). Losses in Families Affected by Dementia: Coping Strategies and Service Issues. *Journal of Family Studies*, 4, 187–199.

Cantor, M. H. (1983). Strain among Caregivers. *The Gerontologist*, 23, 597–604.

Davenhill, R. (2007). No Truce with the Furies: Issues of Containment in the Provision of Care for People with Dementia and Those who Care for Them. In R. Davenhill (ed.), *Looking into Later Life: A Psychoanalytic Approach to Depression and Dementia in Old Age*. Karnac.

Dementia UK. (2023). What Is Dementia? Retrieved from www.dementiauk.org/about-dementia/dementia-information/what-is-dementia (accessed February 2023).

Evans, D. and Lee, E. (2014). Impact of Dementia on Marriage: A Qualitative Systematic Review. *Dementia*, 13, 330–349.

Gutstein, S. (2005). Relationship Development Intervention: Developing a Treatment Programme the Address the Unique Social and Emotional Deficits of Autism Spectrum Disorders. *Autism Spectrum Quarterly*, Winter.

Hellstrom, I. and Lund, U. (2007). Sustaining 'Couplehood': Spouses' Strategies for Living Positively with Dementia. *Dementia*, 6, 383–409.

Henderson, J., and Forbat, L. (2002). Relationship-Based Social Policy: Personal and Policy Constructions of 'Care'. *Critical Social Policy*, 22, 669–687.

Hinshelwood, R. D., and Skogstad, W. (2000). *Observing Organizations: Anxiety, Defence and Culture in Health Care*. Routledge.

Hirschfeld, M. (1983). Homecare versus Institutionalisation: Family Care Giving and Senile Brain Disease. *International Journal of Nursing Studies*, 20(1), 22–32.

Hoppmann, C., Gerstorf, D., and Hibbert, A. (2011). Spousal Associations Between Functional Limitation and Depressive Symptom Trajectories: Longitudinal Findings from the Study of Asset and Health Dynamics Among the Oldest Old (AHEAD). *Health Psychology*, 30(2), 153–162.

Kennedy, H., Landor, M., and Todd, L. (2011). *Video Interaction Guidance: a Relationship-Based Intervention to Promote Attunement, Empathy and Well Being*. Jessica Kingsley.

Lewis, R. (1998). The Impact of Marital Relationship on the Experience of Caring for an Elderly Spouse With Dementia. *Ageing and Society*, 18, 209–231.

LSE. (2019). Projections of Older People with Dementia and Costs of Dementia Care in the United Kingdom, 2019–2040. Retrieved from www.lse.ac.uk/cpec/assets/documents/cpec-working-paper-5.pdf (accessed February 2023).

McGovern, J. (2011). Couple Meaning Making and Dementia: Challenges to the Deficit Model. *Journal of Gerontological Social Work*, 54, 678–690.

Mittelman, M. S., Haley, W. E., Clay, O. J., and Roth, D. L. (2006). Improving Caregiver Wellbeing Delays Nursing Home Placement of Patients with Alzheimer's Disease. *Neurology*, 67(9), 1592–1599.

Moniz-Cook, E. and Manthorpe, J. (2009). Introduction: Personalising Psychosocial Interventions to Individual Needs and Context. In E. Moniz-Cook and J. Manthorpe (eds), *Early Psychosocial Interventions in Dementia Evidence-Based Practice*. Jessica Kingsley.

Murray, J., Schneider, J., Banerjee, S., and Mann, A. (1999). Eurocare: A Cross-national Study of Co-resident Spouse Carers for People with Alzheimer's Disease. II. A Qualitative Analysis of the Experience of Caregiving. *International Journal of Geriatric Psychiatry*, 14, 662–667.

Norton, M. C., Piercy, K. W., Rabins, P. C., Green, R. C., Breitner, J. C. S., Ostbye, T., Corcoran, C., Welsh-Bohmer, K. M., Lykefsos, C. G., and Tschanz, J. T. (2009). Caregiver-Recipient Closeness and Symptom Progression in Alzheimer's Disease. The Cache County Dementia Progression Study. *Journal of Gerontology: Psychological Sciences*, 64B(5), 560–568.

Pozzebon, M., Douglas, J., and Ames, D. (2016). Spouses' Experience of Living with a Partner Diagnosed with a Dementia: A Synthesis of the Qualitative Research. *International Psychogeriatrics*, 28(4), 537–556.

Sceats, S. (2008). The Human Rights Act: Changing Lives. Retrieved from www.advicenow.org.uk/is-that-discrimination/whats-it-all-about/human-rights-fred-and-mables-story,10059,FP.html.

Sinason, V. (1992). *The Man Who Was Losing His Brain. In Mental Handicap and the Human Condition: New Approaches from the Tavistock*. Free Association Books.

Uchino, B. N., Kiecolt-Glaser, J. K., and Cacioppo, J. T. (1994). Construals of Pre-illness Relationship Quality Predict Cardiovascular Response in Family Caregivers of Alzheimer's Disease Victims. *Psychology and Aging*, 9(1), 113–120.

Van Assche, L. V., Luyten, P., Bruffaerts, R., Perssons, P., van de Ven, L., and Vandenbulcke, M. (2013). Attachment in Old Age: Theoretical Assumptions, Empirical Findings and Implications for Clinical Practice. *Clinical Psychology Review*, 33, 67–81.

Waddell, M. (2007). Only Connect: The Links Between Early and Later Life. In R. Davenhill (ed.), *Looking into Later Life: A Psychoanalytic Approach to Depression and Dementia in Old Age*. Karnac.

Wadham, O., Simpson, J., Rust, J., and Murray, C. (2016). Couples' Shared Experiences of Dementia: A Meta-synthesis of the Impact upon Relationships and Couplehood. *Aging and Mental Health*, 20(5), 463–473.

Wright, L. (1991). The Impact of Alzheimer's Disease on the Marital Relationship. *The Gerontologist*, 31, 224–326.

Wright, L. (1994). Alzheimer's Disease Afflicted Spouses Who Remain at Home: Can Human Dialectics Explain the Findings? *Social Sciences and Medicine*, 3(8), 1037–1046.

Chapter 7

At Home in a Home?
Institutional Care and the 'Unheimlich'

I shall begin this chapter with some thoughts about the experience of home. When thinking of the question 'What is home?', I found my mind turning to the experience of going into my parents' home in the time after they died – when the physical place held their presence in everything – paintings, furniture, odd notes – the paraphernalia of life, including apparent ephemera which turned out to have a permanence that outlived them. Even the atmosphere and the air itself seemed to hold the essence of the lives lived there, and yet, to the extent that things felt the same, this was a haunting sense of the immanence of what was lost.

Thinking about it more, I came to this: Home is a physical space invested with personal meaning –it is both of us and beyond us. I feel moments of being confronted by the reality of the separate, independent life of the physical world that I think of as home, increasingly as I get older. How little it changes – the street where I lived as a child, the park I played in growing up. There are small changes perhaps, but mostly, it is shockingly the same – confronting me with a sense of temporality, of the briefness of our lives, thrown into relief by the permanence of the world which goes on without us. Perhaps this is an artefact, the product of growing up in a relatively stable environment. Maybe it would feel very different against the background upheaval of war or displacement; where lives are lived in a physical and personal space that may be catastrophically changed. And yet, even in the most ordinary, stable setting, home is on shifting sands – time and our lives keep moving on, so that even if the external world remains relatively unchanged, one's place in it is not the same. Older people coming into services often convey the sense of living in a world which is not what it was – mourning, perhaps, a world of youth that has been transformed even though they have stayed at home.

Simone de Beauvoir (1972, p. 315) wrote: 'the fact that the passage of universal time should have brought about a private, personal metamorphosis is something that takes us completely aback'.

As we age, we may face the inner experience of feeling just as we always have and yet of not being who we once were – and this can, perhaps, lead to

DOI: 10.4324/9781032636498-7

a sense of alienation which seems most tangibly experienced as a sense of displacement from home, as if swept away by the passage of time, so that, even though physically we are 'at home', psychically we feel we are not. As Kohon (2020, p. 84) describes, Gertrude Stein, returning to California having lived in Paris for years, found her home, and her school, and so much else, were no longer there: 'There is no "there"', she wrote. She had returned to her homeland but had not found her home.

Freud showed that these two elements: the familiar sense of 'home' and the feeling of the unfamiliar, of not belonging, are captured in a single word, *heimlich*. This recognizes their interlinkage, in so far as these are two roots of the same word. The first and commonest meaning 'belonging to the house or family, intimate, comfortable'; the other, something that is hidden which has come to light, that is secret and dangerous, eerie, or ghostly. These two concepts are brought together in a union of opposites: feeling 'at home', we also have, as a kind of shadow, the uncanny experience of dissonance, of something unknown, not belonging. This latter meaning is also contained in, and mostly associated with, the negative of *heimlich, das unheimlich*, or the 'uncanny'. Freud showed us how our minds are both knowable in ways that we had not thought before, but, because unconscious, also unknowable – and this is captured in the concept of 'the uncanny', which is in essence about the ambiguity of something that is both familiar and unfamiliar. The anxiety of the uncanny involves something on the border of what we know and don't know. Freud touches upon personality transformation as a potential source of 'uncanny anxiety', describing primitive animistic uncertainty about whether a lifeless object may be alive – citing epileptic fits and manifestations of insanity which create in the spectator the sense of automatic or other processes at work behind the ordinary appearance of mental activity (Freud 1919).

What about the experience of ageing which is intruded upon by more than the passage of time? When illness, such as stroke or dementia intervenes? Fiegelson (1993) describes how family members of people with illnesses like stroke or other acquired brain damage may find themselves in a situation which has qualities of the 'uncanny', evoked by such conditions which cause an irretrievable loss of capacity that stops short of physical death. So that the partner who was once a source of life and vitality becomes an object that is now both there, and not there. The person is still 'as they were' in some respects but oscillating with a strangeness and a sense of 'death in life' – so that there is the feeling of the loss of a living person. This description is very relevant to the situation of living with a person with dementia, where they, and those close to them, are so inhabited. Where the known, the familiar person, is rendered anew; where the unknown and difficult to comprehend can, at times, flower into something understood and familiar, but where, increasingly, the person with dementia, while containing the essence of who they once were, is variously changed and changing.

Historically, our societal response to the challenge of the disturbing feelings evoked by confrontation with such an existential threat to mind and identity, as in dementia, has been to exile people suffering from the illness from the visible social world. At worst, the 'warehousing' of older people in institutional settings has put them out of emotional contact – such 'homes' often becoming a ghetto of the 'unheimlich'. This is captured linguistically in the very different associations from being 'at home' to 'going into *a home*', the latter phrase containing not a personal identifier but a generic one – not *my* home or *your* home, but *a* home. An institutional home might be said to contain the ambiguity of the notion of the 'heimlich' – that is 'going into a home' is predicated upon a *displacement from home* – from the known, personal setting of the domestic world to an institution, where the context and familiarity of home, which can hold so much of personal identity, may be lost from sight. Given this, what might enable one to 'be at home' in such an institutional home?

Going into a Home

There can be many impressive, technical 'solutions' to the problem of how to help people feel at home in such settings. Some time ago, I visited a residential home that was expensively decorated in a 1940s British Second World War theme – which may perhaps have personal meaning for those who lived through the war, but one can't help but feel, would have limited relevance to a wider population of older people. These days, there are also ingenious 'smart' IT based solutions – with computer generated voices, for example, coming through the ether reminding you to turn off the tap; or tape recordings of relatives' voices, to provide a sense of comfort. But if we think of what constitutes home, it is emotional anchorage that is most significant. Physical space becomes *heimlich* by virtue of the emotional investment it carries. To be 'at home' depends upon our emotional relationships with others. Both developmental research and clinical evidence tell us that to feel secure, we need to feel held in containing relationships– yet, when it comes to institutional 'homes' anti-relating forces are often dominant. Where the 'unheimlich' threatens too much to intrude – as in the psychic challenges of dementia – then our response can be emotional distancing, which may at times be self-preservative and a necessary means of managing the situation. However, this can become a more rigid feature of the institutional culture. In dementia, when emotional and cognitive anchors are being lost, tragically, our institutional response can be to enact and amplify the losses which are at the heart of the disease process. In the worst circumstances, the person with dementia can find themselves living in an institutional setting in which the opportunity for emotional contact and secure attachment with others is so reduced that the emotional context and meaning of their actions and utterances are lost. In this way, the 'institutional defence' of distancing from emotional contact can instantiate a 'death of meaning' in the lived environment of the person with dementia, which prefigures, and enacts, the end point of the dementing process.

This is exemplified in the difficulty in having a connection and a place for family members, and partners in couples, once there has been a move of one of them into a home. Often, in my experience, family are discouraged from being present 'too much' or are encouraged 'not to hang around' – advised not to visit in the first few weeks of the move, as it 'might cause more distress'. And so, those who go into a 'home' can be de-coupled from others, from figures in their familiar relational world, and from emotional contact with staff too, whose minds might otherwise offer temporary shelter, housing for the person with dementia's increasingly fragmented psychic states.

One person who did not have dementia, but whose physical needs were becoming unmanageable at home, described going into residential care for respite, though he feared it would be forever.

> I feel like I am floating above my life. Not anchored. I am at home but not at home, because I am not in charge anymore. I get up to fetch something from another room, and then realise I can't do it. My son decides what I can do – whether I can remain at home or go into care.

'My links feel fragile,' he said. Would he be able to hold onto his connection with me? Could we speak on the phone when he was in the care home, he asked? When he moved into the home, his anxiety increased. He told me, if you saw a picture of the room I am in, it's made to look as if it's an ordinary, nice room, but it's just an appearance. Things look normal, on one level, but, underneath, everything has been taken over by an evil system perpetrated by staff – who look nice, but it is 'only an act', he said. He was living, so it seemed, in a world of the 'uncanny' – where things were, on the face of it, 'homely', but the apparently benign surface of things belied a malevolent force which had invaded his world – giving the appearance of one thing, while really being another. He described in detail all the evidence he had that everything was being controlled by a highly organized conspiracy, a 'system' – involving all the staff – which aimed to harm him.

I thought that this functioned to organize a frighteningly uncontrollable world, where he was in others' hands in the care home, and, worst of all, in the grip of a malevolent, internal presence – which, at one level, was his illness, the cancer, which, as he put it, would impose a final solution. In this, he expressed how frightened he was, feeling himself to be in the hands of persecuting objects, which I, his son, and others, could not save him from. And in this sense, at times, we were felt to have become part of the system that was imprisoning him, and from which he could not escape. Although he seemed entirely gripped by this delusional system, it was possible, at moments, to reach him emotionally. At one point, I said I thought his belief that everything was being controlled in a frightening, malevolent way was his way of making sense of what was happening, when he felt so frightened and out of control himself. He seemed to stop in his tracks. After a moment or two, he said yes, I have a choice, it's like I could let my mind go completely mad. Or I could try to sit it out until I can go home again.

The situation he found himself in, of being moved into a care home at this point in his life, replayed aspects of his earliest life – when, as a baby, his dependency needs had not found a 'home' with his mother. Instead, he had had multiple carers in an institutional home, and had been passed, at birth, from mother to relatives, before going into care. One can only speculate on his inner experience of the early weeks and months of his life, but it is hard not to feel that what we were witnessing now was a contemporary iteration of fears that were deeply held in his mind – breaking through in the paranoid states which so dominated him, as he moved out of his familiar home into an institutional setting.

In his poem 'Old People's Home', W. H. Auden evokes the powerful feelings that can be engendered in us, when faced with the scale of loss, and diminution of functioning, that is lodged in such institutional 'homes' – which house so many of those who can no longer live independently 'at home':

All are limitory, but each has her own
nuance of damage. The elite can dress and decent themselves
...
Then come those on wheels, the average
majority, who endure T.V. and, led by
lenient therapists, do community-singing, then
the loners, muttering in Limbo, and last
the terminally incompetent
...
As I ride the subway
to spend half-an-hour with one, I revisage
who she was in the pomp and sumpture of her hey-day,
when week-end visits were a presumptive joy,
not a good work. Am I cold to wish for a speedy
painless dormition, pray, as I know she prays,
that God or Nature will abrupt her earthly function?

Auden expresses his response to the painfulness of the situation of the loss of her as she was: 'the pomp and sumpture of her hey-day', giving rise to 'cold' thoughts – the wish that 'God of Nature will abrupt her earthly function'. This helps to alert us to feelings that can be evoked when faced with such loss and with diminished, fragmented psychic functioning. Aside from the love and compassion which one can encounter under even the most challenging circumstances, hatred, frustration, resentment, and death wishes, must also have their place. These need to be recognized as, perhaps, an inevitable aspect of what dementia can require family members and others to bear – and yet, such feelings can arouse tremendous anxiety and guilt, as earlier chapters have discussed.

Indeed, in my experience, the guilt felt in placing a family member, or partner, in institutional care can be profound. This can be made worse by the lack of emotional support available, and by the oft-encountered failure to help relatives to maintain a familial role once the person with dementia is in the 'home'. For the most part, such institutional settings do not have a culture which encourages the family to sustain their involvement in the ongoing life of the person with dementia. Once, when I was giving a talk about these issues, a man in the audience put up his hand and asked for a copy of my paper. If he could take it to the nursing home, he said, they might listen to him when he tells them that his wife always gets so upset when he leaves her, and that he wants sometimes to be allowed to bring in a sleeping bag and stay with her. I have encountered many similar examples of people who wish to be more involved in their partner's life in the home, and yet are discouraged from doing so. And so often they have no emotional support with this most traumatic of separations, made worse because it has felt to them to be needed and wished for, because they can no longer cope at home with their partner.

One man, whose wife had recently gone into residential care, referred himself to a couple psychotherapy service. At his assessment interview, he said, 'I wrote on your form that we are separated, because we are – but it is a forced separation.' He conveyed the burden that looking after her had been – though did not complain of this directly. He told me how his children felt about it. They were worried that the burden of care put him at risk – what if he had a heart attack? A couple of years ago, the doctor had asked him, 'If you could move her into care, and you knew that your wife would be happy, how would that feel?' He told me, 'I cried – and it was a relief – so I suppose I did feel I wanted to.' But at the same time, there was guilt at not being with her. 'There is more space in the flat,' he said, 'and in one way, I feel relief that the burden of looking after her has been lifted. But then I see our bed, and suddenly feel the loss of her again. You think that she is there for a moment.'

At one point, he said, 'if only I could be sure she was dead happy' – and then he stopped and looked embarrassed – 'not that I meant to say "dead"'. We explored this. He was dealing with loss – he had lost her. He said that it was like bereavement, but she was still alive, still there. He had gone to a church event on coping with death and he had said to them, 'I am bereaved'. They hadn't seemed to understand this, and he felt that their underlying message had been, 'you are in the wrong place'. He said he had had a similar experience, of his feelings not being understood by staff in the home that his wife had moved into. He wanted to find ways of contributing to her care – and of making reparation to her for sending her away. He told me that the staff at the home had said to him that visiting her too often would make things worse, that the journey was too burdensome for him, and unhelpful for her. He pondered on this and told me that what they had said had stayed with him, as a question. He didn't know whether it was true. As he spoke more about this, the question changed, and he asked himself, 'Does visiting her make it worse for me, because I am reminded of how it was?' To see her meant bringing to life the grief at how she was now, and the contrast with how she was before. As well as the physical strain, this was the painful burden of the journey that he made in visiting her and that he needed support with. It is this challenge, of the emotional task facing such partners and relatives, that tends to be left unrecognized, and unattended to, by our institutional systems of health and social care.

Relatives and partners are often referred to as 'informal carers', whereas professional care staff tend to be called 'formal carers'. As discussed in Chapter 4, 'formal carers' in institutional settings also face significant challenges in having emotional contact with the people in their care, whose progressive deterioration frustrates the reparative wishes, the need to 'make people better', which are part of the underlying motivation for many of us working in the 'caring professions'. One reaction to this can be to retreat from the burden of the feelings evoked by contact with fragmented minds and diminished capacity – and this can be enshrined as a defence within the culture of an organization. I think it is only by recognising and investigating the nature of these challenges – which are an endemic part of the experience of life in an institutional 'home', that we will be able to understand the support that staff need to undertake their roles humanely and sensitively. In Chapter 4 I referred to research that colleagues and I have undertaken (Davenhill 2007; Davenhill et al. 2003) to try to explore this aspect of institutional functioning. To go into a little more detail about it here, in this approach, an observer goes to an institutional setting, observes for an hour once a week and brings their observation to a psychodynamic supervision group who think about it together. This method aims to help us to be more sensitive to the effect upon us of such institutional processes and better able to recognise our own tendency to be pulled into an organisation's defensive culture. It can provide a way in to understanding the defences and anxieties that are expressed in the practices that we witness, as the atmosphere of an organization, and the behaviour of people within it, reveals the unconscious aspect of its culture, the underlying attitudes, values and assumptions, which, though they might remain unspoken, are enacted within the social context. The following account is based on notes made from my own visits to one such institution.

The 'Home'

The home was set in pleasant countryside – slightly idyllic on first approach, a bit like a country house hotel. Once inside, I felt hit by the overwhelming smell of urine and disinfectant, and the thought of such an abrupt contrast between a preserved outer shell and an institutional inside, the urine a reminder that inside contained more damage than the outer appearance initially conveyed.

The layout of the home was open plan, with a central observation point, a lounge area, with small bedrooms coming off it. Along each wall of the lounge was a row of seats. Each time I went, the residents were sitting in the same seats, with a tray on wheels in front of them, positioned too far apart for any interaction to take place. At the end of the lounge area was a large screen TV which was always on, quite loud. There was an atmosphere of waiting, with people facing towards the empty centre of the room, which occasionally filled with staff.

When I arrived on the ward, Mr A, a large man with thick white hair, attempted to get up from his usual armchair located against the lounge wall. A care assistant came to Mr A telling him that he should finish his tea. She pushed him on his shoulder, and Mr A rocked back and forth, and then slid back into his chair. He picked up his mug of tea and made loud slurping noises as he drank it. He then slowly pulled himself up to a standing position again, and was gently pushed back into his chair, with a query: 'Where are you going? Not yet, you have to drink more.' This happened a couple more times, until the care assistant looked over at a male nurse and made a silent appeal for him to intervene. The nurse went over and put his arms around Mr A's shoulder in a matey way, asking him to sit down. He then pushed down on both of the old man's shoulders firmly, so that he had to sit down. The nurse left, commenting 'You'll have to sit down, or you'll fall down.'

Mr A immediately stood up again, losing his balance, then trying to stand. Finally, he managed it. He started to walk forwards, using his tray on wheels for support, like a Zimmer frame. He made it slowly and painfully into the middle of the room, and I noticed that the other patients, who up until this point had been enclosed in their own individual worlds, were all watching his progress with interest. I thought of *One Flew Over the Cuckoo's Nest*, and Mr A's effort to use his remaining strength to defy the immobility that had everyone trapped in their chairs.

The other patients took an interest in his progress, and I was struck by their vicarious involvement in Mr A's struggle for movement and autonomy. By now, he was standing unsteadily in the middle of the room holding onto the tray on wheels in front of him. The care assistant who had previously been telling him to sit down walked past and did not seem to notice. At this point a large group of visiting student nurses came in with the manager of the home. She described the phone system to them in detail. They were standing in the middle of the room at the observation desk on which several phones were placed. Meanwhile, just behind them, Mr A was taking increasingly unsteady steps into the middle of the room. He was a big man, and I felt increasingly anxious, imagining how much he would hurt himself if he fell. More nurses came in and milled around. No one seemed to notice Mr

A, except for the other patients, who continued to track his painful progress attentively.

Slowly the student nurses drifted away, and the male nurse came back. I found myself on the edge of my seat, trying to signal to the nurse with my eyes that there was something wrong. The nurse saw Mr A and called out to him 'What are you doing?' He went across and led Mr A back to his chair. One of the other patients called out 'We're all watching him, not the TV.' Another replied, 'He's the star of the show.' This was the most interaction I had observed between the patients throughout the many weeks of my visits to the home.

From his seated position, Mr A looked up at the nurse with a sideways grin and pushed his tray away from him, as if he were going to try again. This time, however, he did not try to stand up, and very quickly seemed to be asleep. The male nurse sat down next to Mr A and drained a bag, which I had not noticed before, that was now visible on his ankle, just below his trousers. The nurse said, speaking to himself as the old man was now asleep, 'You just keep on drinking, and I'll keep taking the piss.'

A little later, Mr A opened his eyes. The sun was shining through the lounge window, and an occupational therapist came into the middle of the room, swaying her hips, saying, 'Isn't this wonderful, doesn't it make you want to dance? Would you like to dance?' She swayed across the room towards Mr A and said, 'Nice shirt'. He replied, 'Snazzy, isn't it?' The occupational therapist said something else, and Mr A tried to respond, but she moved away without waiting for him to answer. She went into a side room, and I heard her greeting another patient in a similar way. Mr A put his hand to his brow, frowned, and grimaced. He looked pained.

The occupational therapist's comment 'Shall we dance?' could have represented something enlivening, a savouring of what was once enjoyed. But instead, any more real contact was avoided. Mr A did not have a partner for the slow steps that he was able to make, the 'dance', in his efforts to move across the room that he did need a partner for, and could have been supported in. In the face of such restriction, it seemed that the psychic movement needed for staff to be aware of the emotional context underlying Mr A's attempts at physical movement was too great. This raises the question of the unconscious anxieties aroused for younger staff encountering people so much older than themselves, who inhabit fragmented bodies and minds. Excitement and withdrawal into busyness can be used to shield the self from ever-present suffering. Early in the observation, the nurses' absorption in their discussion about the telephone system meant that the painful feelings associated with Mr A's slow and tortuous attempts to imprint his human capacity on his surroundings were left in me, as the observer. The central observation desk became a mechanical area, devoid of real meaning in terms of what could be taken in. This missing feature of the institutional setting is captured in the presence of the empty observation point, representing an 'unseeing eye' – a symbol, perhaps, of the difficulty in this setting in bearing what is there, in front of your eyes. Undertaking an observation of this kind affords the opportunity of trying to understand what kind of relationship to diminished possibilities can be borne by staff, by visitors, and by the residents themselves.

People working in institutional 'homes' are faced with a setting that is filled with anxieties, and they are often the least supported of all staff working in mental health. Under such pressures, it would be very difficult for any of us to maintain the part of ourselves that is able to allow emotional contact with residents or patients. And, although the defences that we have seen operating in the institutional settings described in this chapter may, at one level, feel necessary for the staff teams and individuals working within them, such defences can be more, or less, adaptive and flexible. If there is a wish to change such defensive cultures, it involves freeing the underlying anxieties which are evoked by closer and less defensive involvement with patients or residents within the home, and so such change can be felt to be emotionally threatening, even if it is rationally recognised to be for the better. Staff need support – and above all appropriate containment – to manage such change. It is unsurprising, therefore, that, at worst, unsupported settings can become dominated by a culture which creates barriers to emotional contact. This can have tragic consequences, because, as we have explored in previous chapters, it is this that is needed, most of all, to provide shelter for the psychic states of illnesses such as dementia, where efforts to sustain emotional contact and provide containment may offer moments of coherence, helping people to inhabit a world of meaning in a condition where they are experiencing progressive dislocation of mind and memory.

Concluding Thoughts

In the changes wrought by conditions such as dementia or stroke, fragmented psychic processes inhabit the body that once housed the intact adult mind, and there is a need for an emotionally anchored environment, able to bear and contain projective processes that are increasingly dominant as verbal capacities fall away. And yet, the emotional pressures of the situation present profound challenges, where not only is there the progressive loss of the person as they were, but the need to adjust to how they are now, in their changing state. For those whose partners, relatives, or friends are so affected, there is the *unheimlich* inhabiting of the familiar relationship by the encroaching illness, and this difficulty can be further amplified by the culture of the institution, which, as I have described, can create further challenges for maintaining relationships, following the move into a residential 'home'. Whether we are relatives, partners, or staff teams working in such settings, if our own defences can be less defensive, then we have a greater chance of being able to accompany those who are undergoing the journey into this new psychic terrain a little further, and for a little longer. Despite the profound challenges of the situation, I have often been moved by the efforts of partners, relatives, and staff to sustain contact, holding memory and identity, and striving to connect emotionally with those who are increasingly inhabited by the 'uncanny' presence of their illness. This may help provide a sense of emotional anchorage, if we can recognise that the sense of being 'at home', rather than being dependent on clever technical innovations, relies on the personal capacities of the human beings within our human services – to sustain personal relationships with those in their care, their partners, and their families – and the organizational culture that needs to support this.

I want to close by inviting you to go to the link below to watch a five-minute film of a conversation with a man whose wife had dementia and had gone into a home. He had wanted to stay with her, and he describes the difficulties he encountered; how staff in the home struggled to make space for him and for his relationship with her, but where, despite the challenges, the importance of their being together is clear.

https://d2uydtwelnij2m.cloudfront.net/Dementia+Carer+Experience+Balfour.mp4

References

Auden, W. H. (1968). Old People's Home. In W. H. Auden, *Selected Poems*. Faber & Faber.
Davenhill, R. (ed) (2007). *Looking into Later Life: A Psychoanalytic Approach to Depression and Dementia in Old Age*. Karnac.
Davenhill, R., Balfour, A., Rustin, M., Blanchard, M. and Tress, K. (2003). Looking into Later-Life: Psychodynamic Observation and Old Age. *Psychoanalytic Psychotherapy*, 17(3), 254–266.
de Beauvoir, S. (1972). *Old Age*. Penguin.
Feigelson, C. (1993). Personality Death, Object Loss, and the Uncanny. *The International Journal of Psychoanalysis*, 74(2), 331–345.
Freud, S. (1919). *The Uncanny*. Penguin.
Kohon, G. (2020). Aesthetics, the Uncanny and the Psychoanalytic Frame. In C. Bronstein and C. Seulin (eds), *On Freud's 'The Uncanny'*. Routledge.

Chapter 8

Dying and Assisted Death

> '... it might end, you know,' said Alice to herself, 'in my going out altogether, like a candle. I wonder what I shall be like then?' And she tried to fancy what the flame of a candle is like after the candle is blown out!
> – Lewis Carroll, *Alice's Adventures in Wonderland*

Death and its Anticipation

Unlike an assisted death, which can mean an appointment with death that is planned, and diarised, an ordinary death can come at any time. Remembering the day when, as a child, she realised that one day she would die, Simone de Beauvoir wrote:

> I screamed ... How do other people manage? How shall I manage too? ... When the reckoning comes ... and you are 30 or 40 and you think: 'It'll be tomorrow,' how on earth can you bear the thought? Even more than death itself I feared that terror that would soon be with me always.
> (de Beauvoir 1958, p. 138)

An elderly man I saw for some years in psychotherapy, until he died, conveyed how he felt the constant presence of uncertainty of when his death would come. He felt that might be at any time because there were many different things that were wrong, any of which might kill him. 'But I don't know and so can't really say goodbye to anyone,' he said. He felt alone with this and believed that others wouldn't want to be burdened with his thoughts of dying. In his relationship to his impending death, he moved between different states of mind. At times, he was gripped by a frightening, nightmare world. Sometimes, this would shift, giving way to a more accepting state of mind – which was never securely with him, oscillating, session to session, moment to moment, with frightening images of being abandoned in a state of absolute helplessness.

He had had a very difficult start in life. When he was a baby, his mother had been hospitalised because of her mental health difficulties, which had

DOI: 10.4324/9781032636498-8

persisted throughout his childhood. This, and other physical health problems, had resulted in her being absent from the family for long periods. Despite this, he had managed to be a father to his children and a grandfather to his grandchildren. He had achieved some reparation, and was not, himself, an abandoning father – he had engaged with his family and his working life creatively. Sometimes, especially as illness encroached, the abandoned baby in him burst through – and, at such times, he would feel himself to be rejected by his children and grandchildren. It was at these moments that thoughts of going to Switzerland for an assisted death would come into his mind: 'What is the point? There is nothing to live for – it would make no difference to *them*,' he would say. His children and grandchildren were experienced as uncaring; *they* were the abandoners. 'If I weren't here ...' he would trail off. At these times, especially, his body was a source of persecution to him. He told me how he would set out to do something – go in his wheelchair to the park, for example – but he found it so difficult, and it was cold, so he got a chill. The chill experience was also, I felt, the disjunction between what he imagined he could achieve and the reality of his vulnerability, and the limits of what he could manage now. When he ventured into the world, he was confronted with his impairment of movement. His bodily deterioration faced him with his restriction and incapacity, which became fuel for a familiar, persecuted, and self-critical state of mind. When he felt his body was failing, he would accuse himself of being a failure at everything he tried. This was echoed in his view of the world, the problems in the NHS, war in Europe, which took him back to his experiences as a young man during the Second World War. Like his body, the world felt to be falling apart. I had an acute sense of how hard it was for someone like him – who had done so much and tried to live a good life, making his contribution to the world, to feel that this didn't protect him now. All his reparative efforts over a lifetime didn't enable him to manage his life in a way that wouldn't persecute him too much. It seemed that this was experienced by him as such an assault on all that he had lived by, that it was hard to go on living.

He spoke of his wish to go to Switzerland for an assisted death, and it seemed that the wish to end his life became more of a reality as time went on, and he deteriorated further. He would often say that he could not face going on, and I felt that the question to me was, could I know about this without condemning him? I felt that he had held on to life, despite profound challenges, but he was showing me that now things were different. His wish to bring his suffering to an end did not feel like suicide – rather, that he had endured enough, and the quality of his life was now at such a low ebb and worsening all the time. He was losing the integrity of his bodily functioning, was in constant pain, and experienced encroaching immobility of movement. On one occasion, when he had told one of his carers that he wanted to die, she had said to him, 'And yet you bring so much joy to people.' This surprised him – this picture of himself – as he struggled, so much, to hold on to a sense of his own goodness. And yet, he said, if he thought about it, he supposed he had done things to help, to give good things to his sons, to his grandchildren – to other people ... But so often he felt like a burden, the infant whose mother was unable to look after him, for whom he had been too much. He would speak of his dilemma. On the one hand, he said, he didn't want any treatment that would prolong his life and increase his suffering. On the other, he did not want to let go of his life, and he spoke movingly about his fear of dying:

> It's one thing to feel, when I am in pain, that I want to end it all – but when I'm in contact here with you, and with my imagination and memories – then it is so hard to think of death, and not existing anymore ... No longer able to observe myself, my feelings – not even to think anymore ... I am afraid of nothingness, I suppose.

Sometimes he conveyed to me how in his dreams he was free of his bodily restrictions. One day, shortly before he died, he told me he had dreamt he was exploring the seashore – venturing somewhere new – though it was marshy, and the going was difficult and obstructed: 'I was trying to find a path through,' he said. 'In the dream, my children were there. They were saying goodbye to me and there were some images and memories of my parents.' In his dream, he thought he had died, and it was a pleasant feeling – but then he had woken again to the pain in his legs and the immobility of his body. Perhaps most significantly, in the dream, death was not painful. This had been something he had always worried about: being left alone in pain. In this dream, the atmosphere was pleasant and calm – and he conveyed the sense that he felt himself to be in safe hands, accompanied by good objects. In the end, he did not go to Switzerland. He had, in his words, 'left it too late', and he was not well enough to travel anymore. Before, when he had had the thought of wanting to go, he had feared he would delay too long and become too frail to make the journey – and yet then, when he had had enough strength to fly to Switzerland, he had not been ready to die. He died, instead, some months later, peacefully, with his sons holding his hands. A few days before he died, he spoke about how he imagined it might be:

> It is so hard to imagine dying. Can you understand that? When I am here – talking to you – looking at my family pictures, I go into such a different world. I'm sitting looking out over my garden in the sunshine. Oh, to stay here and bring down the shutters. I am sitting in my mother's chair, and with the sound of your voice, which reminds me of her.

I said that he wanted to feel that his mother was with him and that I would be with him, at the end. He said 'Yes, well, according to Milton that's possible. "The mind is its own place, able to make a heaven of hell",' he quoted.

Then he added, 'There is a dog barking next door, and clouds in a blue sky. And smoke coming from the chimney of house nearby.' I said it sounded like a timeless scene. He said 'Yes, that's how it feels. I feel I could stay here, in silence, and then be no more. Bring down the shutters. Maybe it's a wishful thought,' he said.

People need help to die – a supervisor once said this to me, a remark made in passing decades ago – which has stayed in my mind. In my work with this man, I felt that I was starting to understand what this meant for the first time. Our work together often explored his struggle to find a picture of his own goodness in the world; a part of himself which might protect him when facing his anxieties about his vulnerability and his fears of being in others' hands at the end of his life. He had conveyed a sense of his need to be accompanied, to feel that I was alongside him, as he expressed his feelings about wanting his death. As time had gone on in our work together, I felt that he was more protected by the reparation that he had achieved, the good life he had led – more in contact with his internal good objects. It seemed to me that, over time, the internal balance shifted for him, towards an acceptance and toleration of the anxieties evoked by the prospect of absolute vulnerability, as death drew near, and his dependency increased. Although the idea of travelling for an assisted death was held in his mind for a long time, he had not, in the end, needed to make the journey to Switzerland.

For most of the people I have worked with who have expressed a wish to 'go to Switzerland', this has remained a journey which does not, in the end, need to be realised. Sometimes, however, the imagined event becomes the reality which is enacted. In my experience, people need to be accompanied and helped to die, as much as possible, on their own terms. What this means, in the context of an assisted death, is what I shall think about now.

Assisted Death

> Nobody should ever know, ahead of time, the date of their own death.
> – Penelope Lively, *Ammonites and Leaping Fish*

If you are concerned about a relative who is in pain and suffering and wanting help to end their life, and you google it, the NHS website opens with this:

Both euthanasia and assisted suicide are illegal under English law.

- Assisted suicide.

Assisted suicide is illegal under the terms of the Suicide Act (1961) and is punishable by up to 14 years' imprisonment. Trying to kill yourself is not a criminal act.

- Euthanasia

Depending on the circumstances, euthanasia is regarded as either manslaughter or murder. The maximum penalty is life imprisonment.

Currently, those who live in the UK wishing to have an assisted death must travel, illegally, to find it. Most people from the UK go to Switzerland, and there is a cost to 'outsourcing death' in this way (Parry and Eales 2015). Only those who can afford it can travel there – and for those who can, the price is more than a financial one. They must travel while they are well enough to do so. Consequently, they must die sooner than they might have done, had they had the option of staying at home. Travelling abroad also means that complicated bureaucratic arrangements dominate the last weeks of life. The person who is dying needs the support of family or friends as they will be unable to make the journey alone. Necessarily, given the legal position, any such support must be clandestine. A family intending such a course of action is cut off from discussion with their care team, and often also from friends and other important people in their lives. This brings isolation, guilt – the feeling of doing something wrong. And there is the anxiety of being prosecuted – of being stopped, at any point, the whistle blown: by the bank, who need to transfer money to Switzerland; the travel agents – whom you must pay for a return ticket you never intend to use. These practicalities around assisted death mean that, in the UK and in many other places, it is a premature death – pre-planned and booked ahead. This is different from an assisted death at home, with your doctor helping to end your suffering when the time is right and life no longer endurable – as happens in some countries or states now. The cruellest aspect of the current situation is that you must die early, to travel for an assisted death.

Why are we in this troubling situation? There is a strong, historic societal fear of suicide. Suicide was illegal in English law until 1961 and there are many records, into the 1950s, of people who have attempted suicide and survived, then being sent to prison rather than given psychological help. When the 1961 Act of Parliament changed this, then assisted suicide was made illegal – and still there are many countries in the world where suicide is illegal and responded to punitively. Making suicide illegal does not stop it from happening – and it is no different with assisted suicide. Indeed, in my view, the legal prohibition on assisted death, for fear that, were it allowed, it would lead to an increase in the number of suicides, backfires spectacularly - as attempts to prevent something from happening by banning it so often do. Instead, as I shall describe, the illegality of assisted death in the UK functions to produce an enactment of what it seeks to proscribe. That is, because people must travel to die while they are still well enough to make the trip abroad, such deaths become closer to assisted suicide than they would have done had the person had the option of staying at home. I will say more about what I mean by this in describing a second case example – this time, where the journey to Switzerland became a reality.

What follows is an account by a colleague who wanted to share her experience of what it is like to go through the assisted death of a family member, her father. It is a closely written account, which brings home to the reader the emotional impact of an assisted death on family members. While she wanted to share her experience, she also wished to remain anonymous to protect the identities of everyone involved.

An Assisted Death

'Assisted death' – at least when it involves travelling abroad - is pre-planned and organised. One minute, the person is there, then they are gone – and the preparation, the psychic work of anticipation and accompaniment, of liaison with medical teams – fearing, and fighting, the worst – this journey towards death does not happen in the usual way. How it does happen, or at least how it was for us, for my father and our family, is what I shall describe.

The illegality of what you are doing means that you cannot speak about it with health professionals. In my experience, this meant that the palliative care team, with whom our relationship was not just professional, but in the intimacy that comes with facing death, deeply personal – could not be told about our plans, which felt like a betrayal of those we had relied upon and to whom we felt so grateful. What would they think of us if they knew? You feel you cannot count on the sympathy and support of others. It is, instead, a fugitive experience, which alienates you from the context of home, and 'mother country', and from accepted narratives around what a death should be. Life, so it goes, should be fought for – held onto at all costs, and the battle only surrendered at the last – a heroic 'raging against the dying of the light'. And it feels, from my experience, that a death that is so fought against – accompanied by similarly heroic medical interventions and slowly lost – is what is expected in our culture, refracted through film and media images of the end of life.

What are the arguments for and against assisted death? I don't seek a position on this. The truth is, I am undecided. What I can convey, firsthand, is what it is like to go through this with someone you love. And one of the main consequences of the policy position in the UK on assisted death is that, to enact it, one cannot wait until life is no longer endurable. Instead, it must be planned, and you must travel while you still can. And so, we found ourselves travelling, like tourists, with a father who was still well enough to do so, and, indeed, who seemed to experience a sudden resurgence – a new lease of life – just at the point of ending it.

I wrote this in the days after my father's death. The glare of sunshine, impossibly blue sky, and building heat in the stillness of an early morning made the incongruity of his imminent death impossible to encompass, when burgeoning life was all around us. We were to go for a walk that morning along the Rhine, as we had done only a few weeks before. This time, our father didn't feel up to the walk when we got to the starting point, and we had to help him down the stairs to get to the promenade by the river. We found a chair for him to sit on, looking over the water, from where he could watch us walk. We have photographs taken as we got back to him. Having walked away, we could then still turn back and walk to him – taking pictures and resuming our conversation with him. We have the photographs, and he is laughing and smiling with us; though in one, taken off guard, if you look closely, his eyes look deeply sad, and in another almost glassy – perhaps with unspoken anticipation and anxiety.

We had breakfast then. We talked – taking things from the buffet. Attentive to Dad – having the family conversations we always had. He spoke a bit about his own father and family in India, as he had done more of late. I remember the ordinariness of it. We went upstairs to our rooms, finished packing. Once done, I went to his room and there met my sister. We were busy, though there were moments of pausing – things were said, love expressed. Little things observed.

I saw again the chair where he had spent his last night, legs propped up with cushions, resting on the iron balustrade outside the window. His toes pointing upwards, looking at the bridge over the Rhine, at the buildings, hotels, and houses on the other side of the bank; people, trams, all going about the business of life in the hazy summery day. We had ended the night, a few hours before, in that room. It had, for a moment then, felt more real – that this was the last night; his last, our last with him. He had sat in the same chair, near the window, but facing into the room – with his three children, us, perched in different positions around him. I think we had gone round, in turn, with his saying something to each of us – about our lives, joking comments about his expectations of us. Except it seems too unreal, implausible even, and so memory refuses to make it clear. I remember the vague sense of competition, at having to try to manage my brother's domination of the conversation. Space being filled, avoiding the touch on the shoulder of reality, of awareness; the anticipation of his spirit, not yet departed, but already returning – in a special, private relationship of sorrow and comfort – touching me, reminding me of something. A shadowy sense of having been here, with him and with my mother, before now – in some way that felt to be a return – to times, moments of being together, that may be in the past, or perhaps in the future; somehow crossing from early childhood – and the beginning – to an anticipation of death, the end.

We got the taxi. Harbinger of death taking us through the morning that was already advancing, the day heating up; looking at the map, leaping out to ask the way, retracing steps. That journey could have been any, into uncharted territory, on holiday – in new environs – where you notice the trees, the solitary bird; the ordinariness of the day getting under way. The next question would be, where shall we have lunch? And then we found it. And people came out and helped him. They helped us into a building – a nice, nondescript apartment – with character, a mural painted on the wall of the terrace – by the doctor's father – whom we knew to be dead. It was an Indian type of theme – the motif of the day, the memory of his childhood. Dad showed an interest in it – and gave a proprietorial gesture, as we came up the steps into the apartment and straight into the first-floor terrace, as though this was a house that looked like a promising purchase, or new place to stay, which it was, in a sense, a new place of residence, a final resting place. He commented on the elephant in the picture – now, I find myself thinking, don't they go somewhere particular to die – isn't that one of the things that is peculiar to elephants?

We had talked it over from every angle, over months. In the cafe of the hospital, the day he had first been diagnosed, a rainy January day. Then, further visits, into February, March; taking his temperature, emotionally, seeing how he was feeling. Anxious post-mortems after I had seen him; on the train, on the phone to my sister. Was it suicide? What would our children feel? What would be the legacy of this if he were to go ahead? He wanted our acquiescence, our blessing to release him from the trajectory of increasing diminishment, pain, loss of functioning. In our minds, keeping him from this became an expression of the phantasy that we could save him from death. In his opposite position, we all came to feel there was, perhaps, a fantasy of cheating death: our need to keep him alive, versus his need to keep control, to decide on the time and the manner of his death. I remembered the comment by Penelope Lively (quoted as the epigraph to this chapter) stating that no one should have to know in advance the date and time of their own death. I read this at the time as a comment on the cruelty of execution ... When the confirmation came through from 'The Swiss', as we referred to the organisation involved in offering assisted death, we asked ourselves, was this the date of his execution that we now knew?

The night before we were due to leave, Dad and I had a 'Last Supper' in a restaurant. The Swiss had been disorganised, and agonisingly slow to get back to him with confirmation. He was being made more anxious by their inefficiency. The very thing that he sought to escape from, being vulnerable in unsafe hands, seemed now to be repeated by the very people whom he had chosen to help him avoid this. It was this experience, along with the containment offered the day before, by the very first consultation – after several months of waiting – with a palliative care consultant, that led him, next morning – the morning we were due to leave – to change his mind. We would go anyway and meet the Swiss – but not go ahead. We could have a short family holiday instead. Anxious calls and texts went on all day between my siblings, who were travelling separately, and me. Was it okay? Was he not going ahead with it?

When we met them at the airport in Switzerland, and together travelled by taxi to the hotel, the relief was a physical, visceral thing. The sun was shining. The air – the buzz of a new and strange environment – could now be savoured. The place that we had thought would be hated, a kind of hell, became a heaven. The executioners' land became the Promised Land – of redemption, and relief. We ate together – outside, in front of the Rhine. Old family tensions eased and gave way, having been brought to the abyss, looking into it, and then allowed to go back, to retrace steps. All of this had a profoundly healing effect; an opportunity to be together, a holiday out of time – which would never have been possible, if not for this strange turn of events.

We made a routine of each day, a rhythm which bestowed on the city, on the experience, our own family stamp. Each morning, after breakfast, walking together to the very expensive hotel, where we were not staying, which was across the bridge, on the opposite bank of the Rhine. Its grandeur was more fitting to the solemnity of the death that had been so near. Our father would sit in the lounge, sipping orange juice, reading, or writing messages on his iPad. Dozing, and thinking and communicating with those he needed to speak to, say goodbye to. We children would leave him there and take a tram from right outside the hotel to the large open air pool complex which we had serendipitously discovered. Nearly empty, as the season was not yet quite under way, we would swim lengths and shower, and talk – looking out of the window of the tram on the journey there and the return, taking in the unanticipated life of this strange new place.

We would return to our father, each day, in the lobby of the hotel – where he would sit by the window in a comfortable chair, looking onto the Rhine. He would ask about our swim, and we would talk to him about what he was reading, what we would eat, or drink. He might show us messages he had written – was this the right tone? Or look at this, a moving and loving response from an old friend. We would plan our afternoon, and slowly make our way through the rest of the day. One day we walked up to the cathedral. Another day we took a tram to the museum. We did, in other words, what any tourists might, seeing through the time we had there – life – family life – replacing the death that had been planned.

On the return flight, he was booked onto a different plane – we had expected to return together, without him. We saw him through into security – and then queued to get our later flight. Then we heard announcements – he had not made it to the departure gate. Where was he? He was too slow, could not get there in time and had told no one of his special needs. When he missed his flight, he had to turn to those in authority to help him. He explained his situation – for the first time, publicly vulnerable and in need of help. They put him onto our flight, and we met him, just as we were to embark, being escorted by staff and in a wheelchair. The thing he had not wanted to happen, his disablement, was now a reality –and in some ways, it was a relief. How we laughed as we were whizzed through the crowds in a special assistance vehicle – and were out of Heathrow and in a taxi in a flash.

We had survived – he had survived – and it felt as though now we had him back. He was not going to die, or at least, if he died, it would be sometime hence. We had time with him – and he would have a 'normal' death – we would be able to look after him, to show him our love in this way; and it would not be an execution, with the trauma of knowing in advance, ahead, on what day, at what time, he would die.

The fates had seemed to be with us – saving him for us, allowing us all to be together in Switzerland – arranging for the tram to take us straight from the hotel every day directly to the pool and back to him, in a rhythm that seemed to have a life of its own for the days that it lasted. All these things had been propitious. Life was with us, on our side. And yet from that moment, the fates became cruel. He complained of pain in his back. It was getting worse. He phoned the medical team, who responded quickly. He was scanned and then told that he was in danger of losing all use of his limbs and control of his bowels within weeks. There was no choice but to have further intervention, which he had refused to contemplate before – painful radiotherapy of the spine to give him a chance that they could slow this down.

The radiotherapy itself caused the very things it was designed to stop – and we never had time to discover whether this was a secondary effect of the intervention, which might then remit, or the onset of the symptoms they had predicted from the cancer in his spine. The humiliation and loss of function accelerated alarmingly quickly. Having travelled up to see him on the Monday, I was back again on the Friday – he texted me, asking for urgent help. Something I knew that he hated having to do and would never do except in extreme circumstances. He endured, stoically, with humour, loss of the use of hands, shaking, hardly being able to stand upright – and, worst of all, humiliating loss of bowel function, which he spent hours, somehow, cleaning up himself. The next day, he finally took up the offer of respite care in a hospice. We were planning with him a move to a different town, to a nursing home, where he would be near my sister, who could be with him every day.

I was to drive him up on the Wednesday – but on the morning of the Sunday before, I had a call from my sister. The Swiss had been back in touch with him and had had a cancellation for the following Saturday. It was on again.

Now we all seemed to move, wordlessly, deliberately, but without conscious choice, into a new mode. Time for reflection, questioning, and debating was gone; we were gripped by an anguished pragmatism, making it happen, if it had to go ahead. I travelled up and met my sister there on the Monday and we picked Dad up from the hospice and drove him into town. I went with him to the bank. My sister began at the travel agent's down the road. Withdrawing money, rationalising his accounts – transferring money to 'The Swiss'; comments by the bank staff seemed deliberately ironic – had he made such a transaction before, surely signs that everyone knew what was happening. But, oblivious, the travel agent joked about our holiday, while Dad struggled to sign his name, his hand shaking violently as he tried. Only weeks before, he had been untouched by any of this – he had been just as he had always been.

He returned to the hospice. We all dispersed back to our homes. But the next day, I returned, visiting him in the late afternoon at the hospice – which, beautiful, yet austere, seemed to have changed little from the internment camp for POWs that it had been during the war. He stayed his last night there, and I went back to his house, slept, and then returned in the morning, to pick him up. I remember the grumpiness of one nurse, and another who, when Dad left the room to go to the loo, repeated to me several times: 'He doesn't like to wear his trousers, does he?' This, about the most dignified and dapper of men, our father.

We got him home and my brother and sister arrived. We shopped and packed and did bits of work that had to be finished off, because this was all going on at one of the busiest times of the term. We prepared a meal and decided what to watch on television. We chose something we had all seen before – a film about the ponds on Hampstead Heath. This was close to where my parents had last lived in London – where we had spent the best part of our lives. And the intimacy of the setting echoed the intimacy of the stories of the swimmers, whose accounts were of survival and near death – of finding meaning, the ponds giving sustenance to their lives. For a moment, while my sister and I were in the kitchen, listening to the sounds of my father and my brother talking, it could have been a happy family event 30 years before, with our mother quietly tending to people's needs – and we felt we could sense her presence with us now.

After the paperwork was completed – each of us filling out forms, the doctor checking Dad's documents, brief anxiety about his baptismal certificate, explaining, again, that they didn't give Birth Certificates in India in the 1930s … Practical, familiar anxiety, would the forms be okay, would there be some administrative problem – some unforeseen error; just like collecting a passport and going through your paperwork with a bureaucrat who might find some arcane reason why you were at fault, and could not proceed … Then, it seemed, this was over; satisfactorily completed. Now the bed that we had seen when we entered the room became compelling. Now it is time. 'Shall I get onto the bed?'

I don't remember whether we helped him onto it, but we must have done. I hesitated and held back. My siblings moved to the right of the bed, in his eyeline. I moved to the left, on my own, feeling that I was on the 'wrong' side, that my father was turned away from me. The doctors – two of them were involved now – made small talk, explaining what was happening. They needed to ask him a couple of questions and they needed to film this. It was unobtrusive and I can barely remember these 'facts' of what happened. All that really stays in my mind is the things he said, his comments, his physical shape, the touch of his hand. Although, as I write, my fragmented memory is punctuated by the sudden coming into vision of close-up details; suddenly almost out of focus, as if the camera has momentarily lurched into a magnifying close-up of a hand or a piece of skin, dizzyingly interfering with a view of the scene, the detail obscuring the whole, buffering my recollection.

I held his hand. We held his hands. The doctor couldn't find a vein. She didn't want to get it wrong. She tried the other hand. Maybe it wouldn't work – perhaps now, this could stop after all. Then, she had done it. Now, everything shifted focus to the other side, his eyeline was now the side of the bed that I was on. Dad found a mint in his breast pocket, one of the sweets he had bought in quantity in the latter part of his illness. He handed it to me: 'with my worldly gifts I thee endow,' he said, smiling. He took off his watch – and held it out to my sister. In the delay over finding the vein, he had joked, 'how long would it take, people might be wondering?', as though we were thinking we had somewhere to get to ... He had commented, earlier, that we were going to have to get back to the hotel, to make the plane journey back, three children alone, whereas all he had to do was ... He had trailed off at this point, leaving the rest unsaid.

They showed him how to open the spigot, to let the poison flow into his vein. He concentrated, shaking as he strained to do it. There was only saline solution in there now, they explained. Then, the doctor tipped some innocuous looking substance, from a small bottle into the funnel from which a line ran into the vein on his hand. We pressed closer, squeezing his hands. I remember, as I leaned towards him, he said to me, 'thank you', I stumbled, 'no, thank you Dad ... I love you'. He took up the spigot, and strained to open it, looking stressed as it seemed not to be moving. After a few seconds the doctor intervened; she took it from his hand, saying, 'you have done it'. He rested back momentarily – as though nothing were happening – then he leaned forwards, slightly, and said, 'it is coming ...' – a look of consternation and concentration on his face. Then, almost instantly, he lay back, with his eyes closed – for a split second as though asleep, and I think, though I am unsure, he let out the beginning of a kind of snore, and then, a movement, a kind of brief shudder, as he died. He was still in our hands, his hands in ours. His eyes closed, the side of his face, his smell, all him. But from one moment to the next, from sitting filling in the forms on the desk next to the bed, to lying on the bed, joking with us, an anguished moment of turning a lever, a look and a moment suspended in my mind, before time re-starts, and he is lying in the same place, still, in death. This all passed in a matter of minutes. The incongruity, the traversing of this in such a rush of time, felt impossible then and still feels unfathomable now.

Selfishly, perhaps, we had earlier remarked that – where there is a fight for life, where death occurs gradually, as the illness wins out over life, then you have a chance to begin to prepare. When death comes, it has perhaps already been advancing so that it is anticipated and expected. After he died, many people said that it must be a relief. Well, in ordinary circumstances this may be so – but this was death by design, so to speak, with nothing intervening between being alive – and dying; one turning to the other – day instantly to night.

We sat with him, and barely noticed the police arriving, and the coroner. They shook hands politely, could see our grief and, presumably, that no foul play was afoot. We left while they were doing paperwork, to return an hour later, walking in the Swiss countryside, down a secluded lane, overhung with trees and foliage, sheltered from the sun and the ultramarine blue of the sky. Life was everywhere, butterflies, I remember, birdsong. We went to the village, waiting for ages at a level crossing for the train to pass, eventually someone pointing out to us the footbridge that was right in front of us. We wandered around and then returned. As we arrived back at the apartment, we were introduced to two men standing waiting in the corridor; they were the undertakers, we were told. We held his hands and kissed him again, stricken, and silent. A taxi was called, and we said our last goodbyes; going out again, across the terrace, in front of the mural that we had stood looking at together just a few hours before. The average wait in our local A&E would have been considerably longer than the brief time it had taken us to go from children arriving with our father to leaving there, forever without him.

We were about to get into the taxi when one of the doctors came running down the steps – 'you haven't taken his ring' – his wedding ring. She gave it to my sister. I carried his bag. We had his phone and a few other things – and rode in the taxi back to the hotel, where we picked up our bags furtively, lest someone asked us, where was our father?

I have a picture of him, a photograph which we took on that last sunny morning. My father is sitting by the Rhine in the early morning sunshine. It is less than three hours before his death.

In my mind, now, I think it is clear. His death was an assisted suicide. Traveling to Switzerland, the need to be well enough to manage the journey, had made it that way. A suicide which needn't have happened, if he could have known, ahead of time, that the suffering of his last hours, or days, could have been in his control. If he had been able to choose the moment when he could no longer tolerate his physical state, and had control of the manner, and timing, of his death – then he could have stayed with us longer, until he truly couldn't go on. A booked appointment, while the person is still well enough to travel, means dying weeks, maybe even months, sooner than they might have chosen to, had the option been to die at the time they were ready. This was the case with our father's death. He was still well enough to travel with us, to walk down to the restaurant and have dinner the night before. To eat breakfast in the hotel on the morning of his death. This changes the death – it becomes premeditated choice – closer, I believe, to the experience of a suicide – even though, intellectually, one knows that a parent, partner, or friend would not otherwise be choosing to die now.

My father was dying, in a terminal phase of illness, when living was hard and painful for him. The line between assisted death and assisted suicide is perhaps a fuzzy one – between ending life as someone is dying, as painlessly as possible, and actively killing the body while life is still palpably present. And yet, in my experience, the difference feels immense – assisting in a death when that person whom you love is so evidently alive is a traumatic experience. And it is a trauma that is caused by the current law, which 'outsources death' to Switzerland. A few weeks' more life, this is important. Your loved one staying until they must go: this matters. Not being forced into a calculated, 'rational' choice to plan an ending to life, this is of huge significance.

Concluding Thoughts

As my colleague's description conveys, for a family member there is a profound difference between a death that is assisted at the very end of life – to relieve suffering – and a death that is achieved by leaving home, travelling across Europe, and dying while still well enough to make the journey. Many older people I have worked with in psychotherapy have had the thought of 'going to Switzerland' for an assisted death as an imagined possibility that does not become a reality. In thinking about this, we might wonder: what are the factors which lead some to travel abroad for an 'assisted death', whereas others imagine this, but do not, in the end, enact it?

We must not overlook the importance of the nature of the illness and pain that people are faced with – the hand they are dealt in late life. In addition, there may be unconscious factors which have their roots in the earliest weeks and months of life. One way of conceptualising this is that there is an unconscious experience of the prospect of death, presaged by infirmity and loss of bodily functioning, which revives terrors of early infantile experience. As I have understood it, at an unconscious level, there may be an equation of the vulnerability that death represents with a trauma which has already occurred: the experience of 'nameless dread' (Bion 1962) consequent on failures of containment in infancy. For those with difficulties in this area of their development, the wheels of time may turn full circle, as the deepest anxieties of earliest life are powerfully rekindled by terminal illness and impending death, bringing a level of dependence on others and a vulnerability of the self not experienced since the first weeks and months of life. As this chapter has described, there may be those who, perhaps motivated by such early difficulties and infantile terrors, as well as current illness and pain, decide to make the journey to Switzerland, and others, with similar histories and fears, who, in the end, do not; and there may be a multiplicity of internal and external factors determining any one individual's outcome, including the conditions of contemporary suffering under which any of us might wish to end our lives.

Assisted death was at one time, perhaps, a more ordinary thing – with doctors freer to help people into death at the end of their lives. Now, protocols replace the clinician's judgement and their relationship with the dying person. And consequently, as I have discussed, people who travel abroad, in having to die sooner than they would have had they stayed behind, journey into the territory of an assisted suicide. In previous generations, they might have been able to trust their doctor to help them let go, when the time was right. This is possible now, in some countries and states, where assisted death is legalised. What does a death, where there is greater freedom for assistance from doctors close to home, look like? I recall many years ago, an elderly patient, a former family doctor, describing how, in his earlier professional life, he had made an informal arrangement with a patient, a promise to end his suffering when the time was right. Would that same wish be granted to him, now that he was old and facing the end of his life, he asked?

Freud himself had such an arrangement with his own physician. By the summer of 1939, he was frail and suffering intense pain from terminal, inoperable mouth cancer. As his biographer Peter Gay wrote:

> On September 21, 1939, Freud grasped the hand of his friend and doctor, Max Schur, and reminded him of his earlier pledge not to 'leave me in the lurch when the time has come'. Freud was in exile, having arrived in England months before his death. In escaping Nazi-dominated Austria, however, he was able to 'die in freedom'.
>
> (Gay 1988, p. 651)

Freud's friend from Vienna, Stefan Zweig, wrote:

> [Freud] was very ill with the disease that was soon to take him from us ... As time went by, death cast its shadow more and more clearly over his face ... hollowed his cheek, chiseled the line of his temples beside his brow, twisted his mouth sharply, silenced his lips. But Death ... could not prevail over his eyes and mind [which] remained clear to the last ... That struggle by the strongest will and most penetrating mind of our time against its downfall grew more and more cruel. Only when he himself clearly recognized – he, to whom clarity had always been the prime virtue of thought – that he would not be able to write or think any more did he ... allow the doctor to put an end to his pain. It was a fine conclusion to a fine life, a memorable death even among the many deaths of that murderous time. And when we, his friends, lowered his coffin into English earth, we knew we had given that earth the best of our own native land.
>
> (Zweig 1943, p. 475)

I think this conveys the importance of allowing people to end their lives at a point where the pain of illness and debilitation makes it clear that now, at that moment, in their dying, they wish, and need, to be released from suffering. Such 'death in freedom' is of vital importance for our humanity and dignity, for those who are dying, as well as for those they are leaving behind. And it is with these thoughts, and these images, that this book comes to an end.

References

Bion, W. (1962). *Learning from Experience.* Heinemann.
de Beauvoir, S. (1958). *Memoirs of a Dutiful Daughter.* Penguin.
Gay, P. (1988). *Freud: A Life for our Time.* J. M. Dent & Son.
Lively, P. (2014). *Ammonites and Leaping Fish: A Life in Time.* Penguin.
Parry, B. and Eales, S. (2015). *The True Cost: How the UK Outsources Death to Dignitas.* Campaign for Dignity in Dying.
Zweig, S. (1943). *The World of Yesterday.* Viking.

Index

Abraham, Karl 18n4
Abrahams, Caroline xviii
'Afghan' (Feinstein) 37
age differences and ageing 48–50
ageing: catastrophes of xiv; importance of xiii; imprint of 2–3; losses associated with 21; making use of extra years 1–2; people living longer 1; in reverse xiii; societies hatred of xiv–xv
Ainsworth, M. 77
Alzheimer's disease 57–58
annihilation, terror of, in infancy 4
anosognosia 57
anticipatory grief 75–76
Ashburner, C. 66
assisted death: assisted suicide vs 132; under English law 122–123; euthanasia 123; following death 131; as fugitive experience 124–125; at home vs pre-mature death 123; impact on family members 124–132; last moments 129–130; as more common 132–133; overview xxii–xxiii; paperwork for 129; practicalities of 123; as premeditated choice 131; as pre-planned 124; suicide 122; talking it over 126
assisted suicide 122, 132
attachment: developmental research in 77–78; infant development and 66, 77–78; insecurity 77, 88; in old age and dementia 76–77; recognition of 103–104; secure attachment 77–78
attachment seeking behavior 77
Auden, W. H., 'Old People's Home' 112
awareness: absence of 58; assessment tools for determining 57–58; dementia and 56–59; levels of 70; pictures to stimulate, use of 59
Away from Her (film) 27

Bell, D. 43
Bion, W. R. 23
Birkstead-Breen, D. 41–42
Blue Note 47
Brearley, M. 16, 42, 52
Bredin, K. 67
Bronstein, C. 43

carers: containing function of 63, 94–95; emotional challenge facing 95–96, 114; informal vs formal 114; processing feelings 71; quality of relationship with 65–66, 70; relationships with 63–66, 70; relatives as 63; state of mind of 64–65; support for 70; sustaining emotional contact 65; unconscious anxieties and defences 67–69, 70–71, 116–117
Carers UK 63
catastrophes of old age xiv, 21
childhood anxieties, return to 4–7
clapping care workers xv–xvi
claustro-agoraphobia 6
claustrophobia at home 6, 17
clinical settings *see* institutional homes
Collins, David xvi
communications, of people with dementia 79–80
connections 45–47, 76, 78–79
container-contained model 69, 79
containment: burden of 63; carers and 63, 94–95; containing the container 69; in couple relationships 9–11, 94–95, 98–99; for the healthy spouse 99; importance of 6–7, 17; infant

development and 78–79; projective identification and 79
couples living with dementia: carer's emotional challenge 95–96; carer's losing sense of identity 85–86; case example on working with 85–87; containment for the healthy spouse 99; coping with complaints 10; dementia diagnosis, experience of 97; dynamics of 84; emotional contact between (*See* emotional contact); fear of dementia overtaking both 100–101; government policies 104; inter-connectedness in 83, 92–93; interdependency of 82–84, 104; mourning loss of togetherness 86–87; overview xxi; physical and emotional confrontations 76; predicting move to residential care 92; recognizing attachment needs 103–104; relationship changes 98–99; relationship impacts 82–83; trauma of diagnosis 97; withdrawal tendencies 87; working psychotherapeutically with xxii
Covid-19: age-based triage tool xvii–xviii; ageist comments during pandemic xvi–xvii; clapping care workers xv–xvi; deaths from xiv–xv, xix; UK governments' response to xvi–xviii
Covid Enquiry xvi–xvii
cut off, feelings of being 45

Davenhill, R. 67, 94
death: anticipation of 119–122; awareness of 3–4; consequences of knowledge of 40; death instinct vs fear of 41–42; early life anxieties rekindled by impending 132; evaluating one's goodness in the world and 121, 122; fantasy of cheating 126; fear of 16, 41–42, 51–52, 121; as gradual 4; imagining 121–122; pre-conceptions of 23–24; as a release 15; shaping perception of time 3, 52; states of mind on impending 119–121; unconscious experience at prospect of 132; *see also* assisted death
death in freedom 133–134
death instinct vs fear of death 41–42

de Beauvoir, Simone xiii, xvii, 108, 119
defences: breakdown in 46; fear of 31; no longer holding up 30–33; obsessionality 45; sexuality and 30; withdrawal 43–45
De Masi, F. 4, 16, 52
dementia: frequency of developing 7, 56, 92; internal experience (*See* internal experience of the person with dementia); living with a partner with (*See* couples living with dementia); negative loop of withdrawal 7; overview xxi; potential meaning behind behaviours 9–10; types of 91–92; warehousing older people with xix
dementia care mapping 67
dementia care settings: environment, importance of 64; mayhem and 67–68; observational studies of 69; psychotherapeutic input, value of 66–67; quality of care 71; staffs' unconscious anxieties and defences 67–69, 70–71; unconscious processes within 66–70; *see also* carers, institutional homes
dementia diagnosis: experience of 97; therapist's role at assessment 97–98; trauma of 97
dependency: in childhood 46; in marriage 31; threat of 46
depression: fear of, in couples 50–51; retirement, as trigger to 24
depressive position functioning 5
Deutsch, H. 22–23
developmental positions, defined 2
dimensions of time 40, 41–42
disconnection 39, 45–46
dislocation xx–xxi, 37
displacement in old age: competing demands 50; couples' age differences 48–50; couples and 48–52; external difficulty of 38–39; internal difficulty of 39; Oedipal anxieties and generational 28–29; social context of 38–39

ego functioning 61
Eliot, T. S. 4, 38
embodied experience of time passing 4
emotional anchorage 117–118

emotional contact 9; formal carers and 95–96, 114; with fragmented experience 95; guilt impoverishing 86; importance of 80–81, 88; institutional defence of distancing from 110–111; interdependence of older couples 82–84; meaning-making and 81–82; while experiencing dementia 81–82
emotional distancing, as self-preservation 110
erectile dysfunction 23
eternal youth 1
euthanasia 123
Eyre, Richard 58

failure, internal accusations of 12
fear of dying 16, 41–42, 51–52, 121
feelings, killing off of 45
Feinstein, Elaine 17–18, 22, 37
Fiegelson, C. 109
final journey, feeling accompanied on 17–18 *see also* assisted death
formal carers *see* carers
Forsund, L. H. 83
fragmentation: feared state of impending 13, 16; of the mind 8; of psychic functioning 17; unconscious anxieties of 5
Fraiberg, S. 62
Franzen, Jonathan 63
freezing of time 41–42
Freud, Sigmund: on ability to conceive our own death 3, 23; on ageing 21; assisted death arrangements 133; on decreasing libidinal energy 22–23; on *heimlich* 109; on inner freezing 34; letter to Lou Andreas-Salomé 21; letter to Marie Bonaparte 37; making use of extra years 1; on unconscious' belief in death 3, 28, 41
Froggatt, A. 56
functional limitations, associations between depressive symptoms and 82 *see also* loss of function

Gay, Peter 133
gerotranscendence 46–47
'Getting Older' (Feinstein) 22

Hancock, Matt xvi
Hardy, Thomas 20–21, 33–34
Harrison, Tony 66

Heidegger, Martin 41
heimlich 109
Hess, N. 21
Hewison, D. 34
Holman, C. 66
home: defining 108; sense of displacement from 108–109; *see also* institutional homes
human rights of older adults xviii

imagined non-existence 3
immortality, wish for 1, 43
impotence 23
infant development: annihilation, terror of 4; attachment needs of 66, 77–78; caregiver's responsiveness to 78; psychological legacy 62–63
infantile anxieties 4–5
informal carers *see* carers
inner freezing 34
inner loneliness 16
insecure attachment 77, 88, 92
institutional functioning 114
institutional homes: connections in, difficulty with 110–111; diminution of functioning and 112; emotional distancing and 110; family members guilt in using 113–114; feeling at home in xxii; helping people feel at home in 110–114; human rights of older adults xviii; interactions between residents and staff 115–116; lack of emotional engagement for couples 104–105; as more relationship-minded 104–105; neglecting couple relationships 103–104; observations of 114–117; physical description of 114–115; residents' immobility in 115–116; self-preservation and 110; staffs' unconscious anxieties and defences 116–117
inter-connectedness 83, 92–93
internal experience of the person with dementia: ego functioning 61; external reality overlapping 60–61; staff frustrations with 61–62; theft accusations, making sense of 61–62
internal migration xx–xxi, 52
internal reparation 18n4, 35, 47 *see also* reparation

intimacy in old age xx, 8–9, 20–23, 26–27, 32
isolation 12

Jackson, S. 66
Jacques, E. 39

King, P. 23
King Lear (Shakespeare) 15, 29–30
Kitwood, T. 67
Klein, M: anxieties in older people and 28–30; depressive position functioning 5; developmental positions 2
Kohon, G. 109

Lively, Penelope 2, 11, 39
Living Together with Dementia (LTwD) intervention: case example of use of video 102–103; enabling greater contact in everyday activities 100–101; engaging the person with dementia 99–100; focus of 93; as manualised 101; overview 91; post-diagnosis phase 94–95; psychoanalytic approach 93–94; videos, use of 99–100, 102–103
loneliness in old age 11–12, 16
loss and mortality, meaning of 53
loss and mourning 53
loss and separation: knowledge of our limited time 75; retreat from realities of 42; underlying fear of 25–26
loss of function 26, 126, 128
lost object, internalization of, in psychic world 18n4
Lovestone, S. 66
LSE 92

malignant mirroring 94
manic qualities 51
Martindale, B. 46
Matisse, Henri, making use of extra years 1
mayhem 67–68
McDougal, S. 4–5
McDougall, J. 17
meaning-making 81–82
menopause 22–23
mid-life crises 39, 40
Miesen , B. 77
Money-Kyrle, R. 3, 23, 41

mortality: shadow line and 40; temporality of time 40
Munro, Alice 27

Nirvana principle 41–42
Noirot, Louis 20

Obholzer, A. 69
occupational therapists 116
Oedipus complex 27–30
'Old People's Home' (Auden) 112
oppression, sense of 20–21, 33

parent fixation 62
partner loss 11
partners without dementia: capacity to be interested 96; as containers for their spouse 83, 98–99; containment for 99; emotional challenge facing 95–96; support for 81; *see also* carers
'passing on of the baton' 29–30
Penance (Hardy) 34
physical connection *see* intimacy in old age
'Plain Sense of Things, The' (Stevens) 3
Post, S. 57
projective identification 79, 95
psychic retreats: defined 18n3; from emotional warmth 34; ethereal state of timelessness and 52; internal refugees migrating to 53; state of 11, 17, 42–46; withdrawal into 7–8; *see also* withdrawal
psychic separateness 86
psychological difficulties, unresolved 62
psychotherapeutic input, value of 66–67

Quinodoz, D. 7, 40, 43, 47

Rack, P. 37
reconciliation 15
relinquishment from one generation to the next 29–30 *see also* Oedipus complex
Rendell, Ruth 20
reparation: displacement of 13–14; impending death and 120; internal 18n4, 35, 47; limits of time left for 14; possibilities of creative 15; potential for 35; reconciliation and 15
residential/institutional care *see* institutional homes

retirement: fear of 26–27; as trigger to depression 24
Roberts, Liz Savile xvi
Rosen, Michael xix

Savage, Michael xviii
secure attachment 77–78
self-awareness, dementia and 56–59
self-deception 51
sexual functioning, age-related changes in xx, 26–27
sexuality, lifelong defensive use of 30
sexual longing *see* intimacy in old age
shadow line 39, 40
Shakespeare, William, *King Lear* 15, 29–30
Siddhartha, Prince (Buddhist legend of) 42, 52
Sinason, V. 94
stability, illusion of 43–44
Steiner, J. 42, 44
Stern, J. M. 66
Stevens, Wallace, 'Plain Sense of Things, The' 3
stuckness, feelings of 24–27
suicide: under English law 122, 123; societal fear of 123

Tapper, James xviii
temporality of time 40
Terry, P. 67
Thematic Apperception Test 59

Thomas, Dylan, on death of his father 41
Thornstam, L. 46–47
timelessness: illusion of 44; psychic retreat into state of 11, 52
Tronick, E. 78

'uncanny, the' theory 109
uncanny anxiety 109, 118
unconscious, as immortal 3, 28, 41, 62
unheimlich 109, 110, 117

Vallance, Patrick xvii
Van Assche, L. V. 77
vulnerability and dependency: attacks on 50–51; exploitation of 50–51; return to, in ageing 4

Waddell, Margot 9, 63, 80, 94
warehousing older people xix, 78, 110
Warnock, Baroness 40
Whitehorn, Katherine 39
Williams, Zoe 38
Winterbottom, Michael xv
withdrawal: as a defence 43–45; human tendency to 87; negative loop of 7; *see also* psychic retreats

youth culture xix, 38

Zweig, Stefan 133